Also by K. L. Cook

Last Call
The Girl from Charnelle
Love Songs for the Quarantined
Marrying Kind
Lost Soliloquies

THE ART OF DISOBEDIENCE

ESSAYS ON FORM, FICTION, AND INFLUENCE

K. L. COOK

ICE CUBE PRESS, LLC
NORTH LIBERTY, IOWA, USA

The Art of Disobedience: Essays on Form, Fiction, and Influence

Copyright ©2020 K.L. Cook

First Edition

Isbn 9781948509145

Library of Congress Control Number: 2020932251
Ice Cube Press, LLC (Est. 1991)
205 N. Front Street
North Liberty, Iowa 52317 USA
www.icecubepress.com | steve@icecubepress.com

All rights reserved.

No portion of this book may be reproduced in any way without permission, except for brief quotations for review, or educational work, in which case the publisher shall be provided copies. The views expressed in *The Art of Disobedience: Essays on Form, Fiction, and Influence* are solely those of the author, not the Ice Cube Press, LLC.

The paper used in this publication meets the minimum requirements of the American National Standard for Information Sciences—Permanence of Paper for Printed Library Materials, ANSI Z39.48-1992.

Raymond Carver's story, "Popular Mechanics," appears as "Little Things" in *Where I'm Calling From: Selected Stories* (Vintage 1989).

Manufactured in USA

Cover photo: Charissa Menefee
Author photo: Lena Menefee-Cook
Cover Design: Lena Menefee-Cook and Charissa Menefee

For Richard Russo and Sena Jeter Naslund

THE ART OF DISOBEDIENCE

1   Making Mischief

Habits of Art
9   Habits of Art
19   The One Thing You Need to Know to Writ Fiction: Thirty Theories
30   The Art of Disobedience: Twenty Ways to Misbehave
58   Channeling Voices: On Point of View
83   Describe, Praise, Question: Workshop as Gift Community

Forms of Fiction
117   The Pleasures of Form
125   Every Story is a Love Song
129   The Secret Story: Rituals of Revelation
140   A Family Theme, A Family Secret
145   Narrative Strategy and Dramatic Design
174   The Cyclical Imagination: Short Story Cycles, Linked Stories, and Novels-in-Stories

Under the Influence
201   What We Talk About When We Talk About Influence

206	The Origins of *The Girl from Charnelle*
210	Giving and Taking in McMurtry's West
248	On the Road: The Do-It-Yourself Book Tour
262	Sena Jeter Naslund and the Ecstasy of Influence
289	My *Hamlet*
315	Acknowledgments

"Art is, first and foremost, a gift."

—Lewis Hyde, *The Gift: How the Creative Spirit Transforms the World*

Making Mischief

The best art is always disobedient. The creative works that move us, compel us, provoke us, haunt us, and transform us—the works that matter most to us and that we cherish—break the rules in significant ways. Certainly, characters must act out, act up, transgress, and misbehave. But the writer must also surprise, subvert, deconstruct, and engage in serious mischief, in terms of genre, form, or sensibility in order to make the familiar strange and the strange familiar.

These essays explore not only literary disobedience but also the pleasures and energies of form and genre—including the pleasures of subverting traditional forms and genres—as well as the shaping power of literary and nonliterary influence, and what it means to be not just, as the literary critic Harold Bloom famously asserted, anxious about those influences, but what it means to be, as the novelist Jonathan Lethem has suggested, ecstatically in conversation with those influences and to recognize that every act of artmaking is, on a profound level, "sourced," whether we recognize it or not.

The Art of Disobedience draws upon my experience of three decades spent not only writing, but also teaching and lecturing about the art and craft of creative writing, particularly fiction. This collection owes much to the tradition of my favorite books on writing—essay collections that explore, from a practitioner's perspective, significant and sometimes idiosyncratic issues of aesthetics, craft, form, process, influence, and what it means to spend a life reading and thinking about classic and contemporary literature and trying to write it—books such as Flannery O'Connor's *Mystery and Manners,* E. M. Forster's *Aspects of the Novel,* Charles Baxter's *Burning Down the House,* Margot Livesey's *The Hidden Machinery,* Robert Boswell's *The Half-Known World,* David Lodge's *The Art of Fiction,* Jane Smiley's *13 Ways of Looking at the Novel,* Robert Olen Butler's *From Where You Dream,* and Joan Silber's *The Art of Time in Fiction.*

Earlier versions of several of these essays were published in *The Writer's Chronicle, Poets & Writers, Bloom, Glimmer Train*'s Bulletin, *Now Write: Fiction Exercises from Today's Best Writers and Teachers,* and in invited blogs on the art and craft of writing. Most of the essays are adapted from classes I've taught and lectures I've given at colleges, universities, conferences, and literary centers, especially my primary academic homes: Iowa State University's MFA Program in Creative Writing & Environment, Prescott College, and Spalding University's low-residency MFA in Writing Program. The intensive residencies at Spalding University, in particular, offered me opportunities to distill years of thinking about issues of technique and aesthetics into essay-length craft and plenary lectures.

Some of these essays are short and personal, focused on my own habits of art or the process of making the books I've written, while others are more analytical, operating as broader statements about the crucial significance of literary form and influence, or as inquiries into the work of other authors who have influenced me, or propositions about the way imaginative literature, particularly fiction, makes its meaning and works its magic on both the writer and the reader.

The essays in the first section, *Habits of Art,* have their roots in the process and aesthetics of writing fiction, beginning with more aphoristic entry points into practices of art, theories of fiction, and strategies for intentional fictive disobedience. I also examine what writers mean when we talk about point of view, arguably the most important element of craft for a fiction writer to understand and master and yet an element that both beginning and seasoned writers do not adequately understand. In "Describe, Praise, Question: Workshop as Gift Community," I explore why criticism is more effective when it is descriptive and analytical—an approach informed by my study of artistic gift communities and that has emerged, over the last quarter of a century, from thousands of workshops I've facilitated, letters I've written to my students, and stories, collections, novellas, and novels I've helped my undergraduate and graduate students develop.

The *Forms of Fiction* section consists of essays that meditate on the central role that form plays in narrative art. How do, for instance, boundary genres—such as sudden fiction and linked stories—allow both reader and writer to move in liminal emotional and aesthetic spaces? Are all stories really, at heart, secrecy plots, with intricate patterns of revelation, reckoning, and recalibration? "Every Story is a Love Song" details the evolution of my third book of fiction, *Love Songs for the Quarantined.* In "Narrative Strategy and Dramatic Design," I offer different methods of conceptualizing plot, shape, structure, design, and narrative strategy in scripts and fiction; it is also a detailed formal analysis of *Othello,* the most contemporary and perfectly constructed of Shakespeare's great tragedies. And in "The Cyclical Imagination: Short Story Cycles, Linked Stories, and Novels-in-Stories," I describe and offer strategies for designing the kind of book I most love and have spent a considerable time thinking about as a writer, teacher, scholar, and mentor—books lodged in the gray zone between the collection of stories and the novel. This essay also explores the way our minds are wired not only for narrative but for serial narrative.

The essays in *Under the Influence* investigate what it means to be ecstatically engaged with and even haunted by artistic influences. In addition to an overview essay, "What We Talk About When We Talk About Influence," and essays about the development of my novel, *The Girl from Charnelle,* and my experience putting together a do-it-yourself book tour when I published my first book, this section includes lengthier case studies on influence. In "Giving and Taking in McMurtry's West," I examine an underrated but significant early novel by Larry McMurtry, a writer who grew up in West Texas, not far from where I was born, and who casts a long shadow over most Texas writers. More broadly, this essay explores the work of a major Western American novelist in contentious conversation with his frontier heritage and the literary tradition of the Western—a subject of keen interest to me, given my own relationship to this same tradition. "Sena Jeter Naslund and the Ecstasy of Influence" has its origins in a keynote address I gave on the occasion of the novelist Sena Jeter Naslund's retirement as the director of the MFA Program in Writing at Spalding University. In this essay, I discuss her influence on me personally and professionally, as well as her ambitious career as a novelist imaginatively engaged with her own personal, historical, and literary influences.

"My *Hamlet,*" the final essay, also began as a plenary lecture at Spalding, given as part of the city of Louisville's commemoration of the 400th anniversary of Shakespeare's death. The most personal piece in this collection, it explores my haunted thirty-five year history with this play—as a student, actor, professor, scholar, writer, son, brother, husband, and father.

These essays are inspired by and indebted to many people, primarily my fellow writers, colleagues, and students, with whom I've spent the most time over the years exploring and analyzing these issues of aesthetics, process, form, fiction, and influence. This book is offered in gratitude for their provocative company as we have tried to improve one another's imaginative efforts and to understand what it means to spend a life making artistic mischief.

Habits of Art

Habits of Art

When I was a visiting writer-in-residence at Wichita State University, I worked with ten MFA and undergraduate fiction writers. In our first meetings, I asked the students about their habits of art. The students were surprised by my line of inquiry. Most creative writing programs spend very little time talking, with much seriousness, about process. Craft, we are told, is the heart of the matter. I agree. Craft is where the focus of the conversation should be. Craft can be taught, and there's a lot of it to teach. But over the last few years, I've come to the conclusion that the single most important challenge facing serious writers is not technical. It's psychological, emotional, and spiritual.

As both a writer and teacher, the most important questions for me to ask myself and my students have become these.

How can you, over the course of a lifetime, write not just a few but many books?

How can you finish your work in a way that doesn't drive you or those you love insane?

What kind of process will unleash your best writing and help you traverse, with efficiency and urgency, the space between inspiration and the library shelf?

There are no simple answers, of course. No magic process. There is instead a range of processes and habits of art, some healthier and more productive than others, even if health and productivity don't always result in artistic excellence. The biggest misconception that I've heard when talking to students and fellow writers about their artistic processes is the anxious belief that there is a *single method* and that they are somehow excluded from it or aren't practicing it properly. Each writer must come to terms with how to get his or her work done.

One place to start is by taking an inventory of the kind of writer you actually *are*, as well as the default strategies you rely upon to produce your work. Here is a "Habits of Art" inventory I've been fine-tuning with my students and fellow writers with some good results.

The 10,000-Hour Apprenticeship

This idea, supported by a significant amount of social science research and made popular by Howard Gardner's *Creating Minds* and Malcolm Gladwell's *Outliers*, suggests that it takes 10,000 hours of serious, deliberate practice to achieve basic-level mastery of any kind in any discipline. So, for instance, as a writer, it would take about ten years of practicing three hours every day or five years of forty-hour work weeks to master your subject and to reach this bottom rung of the mastery ladder. Let's say that a typical

MFA degree equals twenty-five hours a week for fifty weeks a year over a two-year period. That translates into roughly 2,500 hours spent on serious reading and writing. Or about a quarter of the way through an apprenticeship.

How far along are you in your mastery? What discipline can you impose on yourself to more quickly develop your proficiency as a writer?

Discipline: Routines & Rituals

All artists develop, consciously or unconsciously, routines and rituals that allow them to create their work. Some writers take a more workmanlike approach—setting daily or weekly page goals or quotas for themselves, or writing at the same time every day, or breaking up their tasks into manageable units ("bird by bird," as Anne Lamott suggests in her book with that title). Other writers depend more on mystery—relying on inspiration, intuition, or even chaos in order to complete their work. These writers tend to eschew routines and thrive on adrenaline, and sometimes they may perfect a kind of crisis-management or damage-control approach to art-making. Still others find ways of marrying the approaches, trusting the muse to favor the prepared.

What kinds of routines and rituals do you employ? What kinds of routines and rituals might help you generate consistently strong work? Are you able to produce your best work through regular routines, or does your best work emerge from inspired binges? Are temporary periods of crisis management and damage control necessary parts of your ritual?

The Teaching Emotion: Kindness & Cruelty

In his play, *Zoo Story*, one of Edward Albee's characters says, "I have learned that neither kindness nor cruelty by themselves, independent of each other, creates any effect beyond themselves; and I have learned that the two combined, together, at the same time, are the teaching emotion." The best artists find a balance. They know when it's necessary to be kind to themselves in order to coax the muse from its hiding place. They also know when to crack the whip, imposing discipline and high standards for quality. Productivity arises from this balance.

Where do you fall on this continuum in terms of your process for creating work? How might you adjust these extremes in order to increase your productivity, improve the quality of your work, and maintain some sense of sustainability in your process?

Accountability: Bribes & Threats

The Danish writer Isak Dinesen (Karen Blixen) advised, "Write a little every day, without hope, without despair." Creative writing—any art form really—is notoriously difficult because the world is not expecting you to produce it, so you have to provide your own intrinsic and extrinsic motivation. Most writers have ways of holding themselves accountable—both for producing work and for its quality. Some, like Dinesen, work slowly and regularly with an even-tempered sensibility. Other writers impose what I call bribes and threats, often in small ways: promising yourself a nice walk with the dog or a chocolate bon-bon after a crucial scene or stanza has been written, or not allowing yourself a coffee break until a section of work is finished. Others rely on friends, colleagues, editors, or agents to keep them accountable.

My friend, Joseph Schuster, shared this anecdote about the lengths he went to threaten himself to produce: "I once offered to pay a ransom to force myself to write by making out a post-dated check to an organization I abhorred and giving it to a friend with instructions that he should send it off if I didn't produce fifty pages on my novel within two months. I made it, by the skin of my teeth, by writing thirty-five pages on the day before the deadline."

How do you hold yourself accountable for doing your work? Are you an even-tempered, Dinesen-like writer? Or do you need intrinsic and extrinsic motivators, bribes and threats, to produce your work? If so, what are your bribes and threats? Do they work for you?

Excess & Scarcity

Some writers are creatures of excess and others of scarcity. Creatures of excess need to write a great deal in order to figure out what they mean. ("How can I tell what I think until I see what I say?" E.M. Forster famously asked.) These writers tend to produce work quickly, but the revision process is slower and often frustrating, involving cycles of writing, cutting, and polishing, followed by more writing, cutting, and polishing. Revision is primarily a matter of endless expansion and contraction. Other writers are reluctant to put a word down on paper unless it's the exact word—*le mot juste*, as Gustave Flaubert famously quipped. These writers tend to be more cautious and contemplative, rigorously perfecting every sentence before going on to the next. The original composing process is slower and often indistinguishable from the revision process.

Are you a creature of excess or scarcity? Are you comfortable with the method you use to compose work? Have you made peace with your temperament? Would it help you to attempt a project using the opposite approach?

Peacemakers & Tricksters

Some writers strive toward harmony in their writing, valuing order over chaos, peace over conflict, construction over deconstruction. Other writers have a darker, trickster impulse that finds energy in deconstructing false narratives, correcting fools, causing mischief, and depicting the ways in which people misbehave.

Does your energy and power as a writer come from a constructive or deconstructive impulse? Might it help you to strive toward more mischief and disorder in your work if you're a peacemaker or greater harmony and aesthetic order if you're a trickster?

Single-Project vs. Multi-Project Writers

Writers tend to fall into two camps in terms of productivity. There are serial monogamists, who work persistently on a single project from conception through the final draft, not allowing themselves the luxury of indulging in another major project until the first one is completed. And there are writers (like me), who like to have multiple projects in the hopper at the same time, letting them cross-pollinate. Writers who focus persistently on one project at a time tend to finish individual works more consistently while multi-project writers never have an excuse for writer's block.

Are you a single- or multi-project writer? What are the challenges or advantages for you of being one type or the other?

Writing as a Gift

In *The Gift: How the Creative Spirit Transforms the World*, his groundbreaking study of the relationship between gift cultures and the artistic process, Lewis Hyde argues that "The artist works … from that part of our being which is a gift and not an acquisition. To speak of our talents as gifts distinguishes them from those abilities that we acquire through the will…. Men or women of talent must work to perfect their gifts, of course; no one is exempt from the long hours of practice. But to set out to acquire the gift itself through work is like trying to grow an extra hand, or wings. It can't be done."

Hyde suggests that artists owe it to themselves, and the communities they write for, to share their gifts. To not do so is a kind of sacrilege. What is your relationship to your gift or talent? Do you feel you have an obligation to it? If so, what is the nature of that obligation and relationship?

Credos & Missions

A significant turning point in the growth of most writers comes with the discovery of subject matter that is galvanizing. Sometimes the writer consciously courts subject matter or a mission; sometimes subject matter or a mission seems to find the writer. The poet Tony Hoagland said that he began as a confessional poet and then aimed himself toward the social. Some writers feel a special need to give voice to a marginalized community or minority group or region. John Updike said he wanted to be a chronicler of the surface beauty of the world and everyday epiphanies.

Some writers adhere to an art-for-art's-sake credo with a concentration on the aesthetic value of the work. Other writers believe the goal of writing is not artistic expression but deep communication (emotional and/or intellectual) with the reader.

Do you have a conscious credo or mission? What galvanizes you as a writer? Which writers do you admire most, and why do you admire them? Can you name your subject or the tradition in which you plan to work? Is aesthetic expression or the process of communication more important to you?

What Are Your Next Three/Five/Ten Stories/Poems/Plays/Screenplays/Books?

"Whatever you do, or dream you can, begin it," the German writer Goethe wrote. "Boldness has genius, power, and magic in it." Generating not only ideas but actual titles, descriptions, and language for future projects can be an energizing process. If you write down your next three (or five or ten) projects, will you be more likely to complete the first one in order to get to the second one, and so on? Can this be more than a glorified to-do list, but rather a way to envision your life's work?

I realize that such self-reflective "inventories" may at first appear reductive or even counterproductive. Conventional wisdom tells us the more you talk or even think analytically about your process, the less you produce. I don't believe that myth anymore. In addition to absorbing as much craft as possible, the best thing you can do, as a writer, is to figure out the kind of writer you are, the habits of art you rely on, and whether or not those habits reinforce your ability to do your best, most original work over a lifetime. Understanding and refining your process, I've come to believe, is actually just as important as understanding and refining your technique.

The One Thing You Have to Know to Write Fiction: Thirty Theories

I am frequently asked to boil down the art and craft of writing fiction into a simple aphorism or sound bite. Or I'm asked by some of my more pragmatic friends or by students and colleagues from other academic disciplines about the purpose and aim of fiction and literature in general—why it's important, why they should care. Over the years, I've answered this question in different ways, sometimes depending on which literary theory I was studying, sometimes depending on the specific idiosyncratic project I was puzzled by, sometimes depending on the person with whom I was conversing. So I now have a list.

What is the one thing you have to know to write fiction? Here is a month's worth of answers.

1. Something Happens to Someone

For most readers, a story isn't a story unless something happens to someone. It sounds simple. It's not.

2. The Inner Life of Characters

If poetry is the province of language and metaphor, if nonfiction is the province of fact and idea, if drama is the province of external action, then fiction is the province of character, the province especially of the inner life. All the primary tools of fiction—point of view being the most essential—are tools that help the writer depict and reveal character. The main questions we tend to ask of a story in workshop—"Whose story is it? What's at stake?"—focus attention on the fact that fiction is about revealing how we think, feel, perceive, remember, and make sense of the world.

3. Transformation

Another central argument of storytelling is that the "something that happens to somebody" must be transformational. *How does the character change?* The change may be outward or inward, major or minor, but without change, a story is not a story; it's merely a sketch. (A variation on this idea of transformation is that the story depicts the character's *last opportunity for change.*)

4. Epiphanies

For many readers, the character's transformation must not simply be an external change—a reversal of fortune, for instance, or death—but an *internal transformation.* Most modernist and contemporary fiction focuses on the way characters reach a new, transformative understanding about themselves, or a new understanding of the world. James

Joyce, especially in his theory about the epiphany, argued that fiction is always about the movement toward *revelation*.

5. CAUSALITY

E. M. Forster, in *Aspects of the Novel,* famously made a distinction between narrative and plot. He said that if we write, "The king died, and then the queen died," we have a narrative—that is, a record of the sequence of events. But if we instead write, "The king died, and *then* the queen died of grief," we have a plot. The key ingredient is causality. "This happened and this happened and this happened" is not compelling storytelling; it is simply narrative sequencing. Whereas, "This happened *because* that happened, which in turned *caused* this other thing to happen" is at the heart of all meaningful storytelling.

6. DESIRE AND FEAR

The central dynamic of all stories is the interplay between desire and fear. Desire is what drives the characters forward. Fear is what holds them back. How characters negotiate those two emotions will determine the central theme of the story.

7. YEARNING

In *From Where You Dream,* Robert Olen Butler argues that the art of fiction is really the art of yearning because fiction is about humans, and humans are "yearning creatures." We only care about characters when we see them in the act of *wanting* something or somebody badly. He suggests that the verbs "desire" and "want" don't accurately capture the true spirit of fiction. "Yearning," he suggests, is a word that captures our deepest human desire—a combination of the erotic, spiritual, psychological, and physical. Plot, he argues, arises from thwarted yearning.

8. To Entertain and Teach

The traditional aim of fiction and all art for that matter—as the Nobel Prize Laureate Isaac Bashevis Singer, among others, tells us—is to entertain us and to teach. In that order.

9. Self-Proclaimed False Narrative

Storytellers are always in the process of exposing false narratives and replacing them with more authentic and complex ones. History, politics, and literature are fierce battlegrounds for control of the narrative. Fiction, as a self-proclaimed false narrative, a made-up story, argues for *felt* authenticity and authority.

10. Imaginative Empathy

The purpose of literature is to promote compassion and empathy. The major decision for you as a fiction writer is to choose whose life you will show the reader. Even if the depiction is critical, that choice is—or should be—an act of imaginative empathy.

11. Confrontation with an Other

John Gardner, in *The Art of Fiction,* suggests that there are two primary stories: a hero sets out on a journey and a stranger comes to town. Both kinds of stories are about confrontations with someone or something that's foreign. How we make sense (or fail to make sense) of that confrontation with the *other* is the primary goal of the fiction writer.

12. Journeys

Joseph Campbell, in his landmark cross-cultural study of myth, *The Hero with a Thousand Faces,* suggested that every significant story in every culture is really a journey narrative, which he divided into twelve parts. The journey narrative begins with a hero leaving home in search of some kind of treasure (a tangible or symbolic treasure, knowledge, or wisdom) and ends with the hero failing or succeeding and then returning to his or her community to share the treasure (that is, the story) of what he or she learned.

13. Vivid and Continuous Dream

John Gardner also said that the primary job of the fiction writer is to create "a vivid and continuous dream in the reader's mind." Like a dream, the story doesn't have to make logical sense or be easily boiled down to a moral precept or simple epiphany. Fiction should capture the complexity and mystery of *felt* experience, in all its familiarity and strangeness, and do so through a rich evocation of sensory detail. Dreams don't always have clear meanings. Dreams are powerful because of their vividness, urgency, and inscrutability—because of the way they arouse, move, scare, seduce, baffle, and haunt us.

14. Moral Arena

Fiction is a moral arena in which the writer dramatizes humans grappling with the complexities of good and evil, and the anguish and implications of moral choice. We learn how to behave properly, morally, ethically, and compassionately by reading stories about how characters deal with the most challenging dilemmas of their lives and the consequences of their choices.

15. Initiation→Conflict→Resolution

All stories are not just about beginnings, middles, and ends, but rather initiations, conflicts, and resolutions. This process is what the characters go through. It's also what the reader goes through.

16. Ritual of Revelation

All stories are really about the way secrets are kept or exposed, and what the consequences are of that suppression or revelation. Plot is about a secret that leads to a revelation (or the threat of revelation), which results in a reckoning, which then leads to a physical, emotional, psychological, or spiritual recalibration for the characters and, by extension, the reader. All stories spring from this great aquifer.

17. The Individual Against the World

E. L. Doctorow, the great fiction writer and essayist, suggests that the "scale of a story causes it to home in on people who, for one reason or another, are distinct from their surroundings—people in some sort of contest with the prevailing world."

18. Let's Misbehave

All dynamic fiction is disobedient and subversive and must reveal the author and/or characters in acts of transgression, misbehavior, or deconstruction. Fiction is not for do-gooders. As writers and readers, we are most deeply engaged when we see characters in defiance of an established norm of behavior. Our interest will also be engaged by writers who misbehave in their treatment of their subjects—through style, structure, form, and sensibility.

19. Making Strange: Defamiliarization

The Russian literary critic and writer Viktor Shklovsky argued that the primary purpose of art is to "defamiliarize" us. Artmaking is an act of "making strange." The writer engages our attention by making a strange world seem eerily familiar or by making the familiar seem disorienting and strange. The writer's job is to make us see the world anew through this process.

20. The Art of Time

Narrative is a *temporal* medium. That is, all stories are constrained and defined by time. Stories happen "once upon a time." The art of fiction—the art of all narrative—is really about the navigation of characters *through* time, *in* time, and *over* time.

21. Love Songs

We may disparage the idea of the love story as hokey, but in reality *every* story is a love story. Every story is a love *song*—indebted to odes, ballads, anthems, arias of seduction, pain, harmony, or suffering. We don't engage deeply with people, places, ideas, or things unless we care deeply about them—or are saddened or enraged by threats to their existence. A story is an extended song embodying and giving voice and music to that love or the threat to what we love.

22. Betrayal

All stories are about betrayal—how we cope with either being betrayed or betraying others.

23. Submerged Communities

In *The Lonely Voice,* Frank O'Connor suggested that stories are primarily the domain of "submerged population groups" or submerged communities—those individuals and subcultures that, for whatever reasons, exist at the fringes of society.

24. Chaos→Order

In James Baldwin's great story, "Sonny's Blues," the narrator says, "The man who creates the music [or writes the stories] is hearing something else, is dealing with the roar rising from the void and imposing order on it as it hits the air. What is evoked in him, then, is of another order, more terrible … and more triumphant.… And his triumph, when he triumphs, is ours." The writer's job is not to create chaos but rather to depict it and to impose order on it so that it is both comprehensible and beautiful.

25. The Aesthetics of Suffering

At the end of "Sonny's Blues," Baldwin's unnamed narrator also says, "For, while the tale of how we suffer, and how we are delighted, and how we may triumph is never new, it always must be heard. There isn't any other tale to tell, it's the only light we've got in all this darkness." The most esteemed stories in our lives are tragedies that explore the aesthetics of suffering.

26. Character+Plot+Theme+Language

All stories, as Aristotle taught us, are about the interplay between four dynamic narrative elements: character, plot, theme, and language. A fiction writer may have a particular strength, but great fiction is rich in *all* four elements.

27. Literary Environments

Fiction is always about a deep sense of place (or the absence of place) and the way characters inhabit, mourn for, celebrate, defend, or are in conflict with notions of home and foreignness. Genre fiction tends to encode assumptions about the characters', readers', and writers' relationship to environment. Westerns, for example, dramatize the negotiation between civilization and wilderness. Horror and ghost stories explore sites of trauma. Noir fiction explores the moral and environmental ambiguity of urban landscapes. Science fiction, fantasy, and dystopian narratives frequently critique the failures of environmental stewardship. Fiction is not only about something that happens to someone, but about something that happens to someone somewhere. The *somewhere* matters.

28. Relationship Not Character

Stories are not about characters. They are about relationships. It's a mistake to focus so much attention on creating fascinating, compelling, complex characters.

Instead, concentrate on creating fascinating, compelling, complex relationships *between* characters.

29. STORY AS SENSEMAKING

We turn to storytellers who can best help us make sense of the nonsensical, simplify the complicated, illuminate the mysterious, contextualize the confusion, and decipher the indiscernible.

30. BENCHMARKS FOR GREATNESS

John Gardner argues for these benchmarks to judge the quality of fiction: (1) it creates a *vivid and continuous dream* in the reader's mind; (2) the *emotional stakes* are high; (3) the *intellectual stakes* are weighty; (4) the writer tells the story with both *eloquence and economy*; and (5) there is always an element of irreducible s*trangeness.*

The Art of Disobedience: Twenty Ways to Misbehave

Too much fiction, too much literature suffers from niceness, an unwillingness to hurt feelings, an unwillingness to offend. Niceness is a species of self-censorship—writers afraid to let their characters think, say, or do the unthinkable, the unsayable, the undoable because they don't want their friends, family members, or colleagues to think that they share their characters' desires, thoughts, feelings, or words. Too much fiction also seems to be written out of a desire on the part of the writer to appear to be doing something socially significant. When a piece of literature, when any art, begins to resemble the classroom or the church or the soapbox, it has lost its urgency as art.

Do-gooding is the opposite of art. We don't still read *Paradise Lost* because of Milton's desire to "justify the ways of God to man," as he claimed was his intention; we read it because of the eloquent and persuasive charisma of Satan, that greatest of all vengeful angels. We read or watch *Othello* in large part because of Iago's inexplicable, giddy malevolence and the chaos he unleashes in others. Hamlet fascinates us not because he ponders the universe and has beautiful things to say about the firmament and the quintessence of dust, but because he vows revenge, is mean to his girlfriend, talks smack to his mother and stepfather, can't seem to make up his mind, and pretends to be—and at times seems to actually go—crazy.

Literature's real subject is always disobedience, a kind of misbehavior that can come in the form of an attack, a seduction, a puzzle, a paradox, a joke, a prayer, or a quiet refusal to participate. "I prefer not to," Bartleby the scrivener says, in what turns out to be a radically subversive act. Our goal as writers is to enthrall the reader. That is, in fact, the primary virtue of any art. But the word "enthrall" has a double meaning. It means to cast a spell, but it also has a more insidious definition: to hold in bondage.

Figuring out the ways in which an author is misbehaving is the first step to articulating not only what obsesses that writer but what is distinctive about his or her work. As a writer, disobedience is your duty and your calling. Here are twenty ways, as a fiction writer, to disobey. The first ten concern character, subject, and sensibility, and the second ten concern narrative strategy, form, and genre.

Character, Subject, Sensibility

1. Shatter Taboos and Sacred Cows

In a tabloid culture, in which any human depravity can be seen on cable television or the internet, what can really be called "misbehavior"? What is the difference between mature and immature misbehavior? Or rather, what's the difference between the artist and the hack? What is your subject matter, your great theme or obsession? What haunts your work or makes you angry? What sharpens your voice, makes you want to speak up? What is your guilty pleasure? What is taboo for you personally to talk about: adultery, religion, politics, sexuality, cannibalism, slaves owning slaves, your love for the derelicts in your life?

The key here, I think, is to create the context in which the misbehavior in your work can be understood, the norms against which it feels disruptive or transgressive. Adultery, even in Hawthorne's day, wasn't the religious and criminal offense he depicts in *The Scarlet Letter*. The spiritual torment of his characters can only be understood within a Puritan context, which was historical even for Hawthorne. An honest and explicit examination of sexual life was the great unexamined material for the modernists such as D. H. Lawrence, Anaïs Nin, Henry Miller, and James Joyce, all of whom suffered decades of censorship because of their willingness to write about it. Although we live in a literary, cultural, and political age in which we can treat any subject explicitly, what, I wonder, can't we write about? What is too private? Or too public? What context must we establish in order to suggest the emotional, ethical, and spiritual seriousness of the transgression?

2. Exploit the Sins, Crimes, and Misdemeanors

When creating characters, follow the misbehavior. Allow your imaginary people to commit crimes or sins. Have them betray one another, debauch themselves, indulge their worst impulses. Have them grapple with their past mistakes. Let them loose. In his novel, *Love Me,* Garrison Keillor—a writer best known for his long-running NPR radio show, *The Prairie Home Companion,* especially his nostalgic, homespun, G-rated stories about Midwestern Lutheran goodness—depicts a novelist trying to figure out how to break out of his writer's block: "I read a book," the narrator of the novel says, "called *How to Write Your Novel in Thirty Days* and one paragraph jumped up and kicked me in the butt: 'The most visceral and vital writing is about bad people and allows the reader to see that We Are Them. For reasons having mostly to do with arrogance and stupidity, young writers waste years attempting to impersonate goodness and inner peace. Bad move. What you really want to write about is greed, anger, pillage, thievery, corruption, eye gouging, meanness, shameless groveling, that sort of thing. And lust. Always lust. *He couldn't help himself, once he looked into those dark eyes. He kissed her again and again. They fell to the floor in an embrace. Oh my God, she said.* Forget about goodness. Kahlil

Gibran did that already. The world doesn't need more Bill Moyers…. Unbutton that shirt. Unzip those pants.'"

3. The Secret Story

Trust in the power of secrets. Create secret lives for your characters. Plot is about the suppression, revelation, and reckoning of the secret lives of characters. A story without secrets is not a story. William Faulkner said that the only tale worth telling is "the human heart in conflict with itself," a statement that implies a fundamental belief in the power of secret lives. Anton Chekhov, in his most iconic story, "The Lady with the Pet Dog," has his middle-aged protagonist realize that "through some strange, perhaps accidental, conjunction of circumstances, everything that was essential, of interest and value to him, everything in which he was sincere and did not deceive himself, everything that made up the kernel of his life, was hidden from other people." That quote should be, I believe, a mantra for writers.

Our most cherished novels, stories, plays, and films are about secrecy and revelation. Narrative serves to expose the protagonist's secret life. Think of Gatsby, Willy Loman, Blanche Dubois, Emma Bovary, Anna Karenina, Joe Christmas, Quentin Compson (almost any Faulkner character in fact), Lord Jim, the unnamed captain who is hiding his stowaway in *The Secret Sharer*. Most of Poe's characters—not to mention those of Dickens, Virginia Woolf, James Joyce, Joyce Carol Oates, Toni Morrison, and Alice Munro.

We all live secret lives. Plot is about the revelation (intentional or accidental) of those secrets and the comic or tragic reckoning of that revelation. Let your stories animate that dilemma.

4. Negative Capability:
Ventriloquists and Chameleons

The Romantic poet John Keats argued that the most valuable gift a writer can have is what he called "negative capability," which he claimed was a writer's talent for "being in uncertainties, Mysteries, doubts without any irritable reaching after fact & reason." He was talking about Shakespeare when he said this, and what he was marveling over was Shakespeare's ability to deeply inhabit and speak in the voice of so many radically different characters. In order to make your work misbehave, in order to feel the danger in your own writing, you must create and inhabit characters who challenge your own beliefs, who are distinctly and convincingly different from you. That means you must become a master ventriloquist, actor, and chameleon.

What we find so compelling about the work of Charles Dickens or William Faulkner or Louise Erdrich or Joyce

Carol Oates (not to mention actors such as Meryl Streep and Daniel Day-Lewis) is the sheer audacity they exhibit in channeling the voices and spirits of their characters. I want to urge you to tell your semi-autobiographical coming-of-age novel from your mother's perspective or your father's or your suicidal aunt's. Or as the novelist Robert Boswell suggests in *The Half-Known World*, "In situations where you see a clear injustice, situating the story in the point of view of the aggressor will more likely permit you to find the full human dimensions of both the victim and the aggressors, which in turn will give you the opportunity to avoid moralizing melodrama and achieve a work of literature that is also a political statement."

The great advantage that the fiction writer has over the memoirist is this license to become someone else. Both as a writer and as a reader, this audacity is both dangerous and energizing.

5. Negative Capability: Be Mean

Create characters who will call out and investigate your protagonists' faults, who can see into their souls, who will deliver a reckoning, who aren't afraid to be mean. The late poet Tony Hoagland, in his essay entitled "Negative Capability," turns Keats' famous aesthetic on its head and makes a compelling argument for the aesthetic value of meanness. Though he's talking about poetry, it applies to fiction and other genres just as well. "Meanness," he says, "the very thing that is unforgiveable in human social life, in poetry is thrilling and valuable. Why? Because the willingness to be offensive sets free the ruthless observer in all of us, the spiteful perceptive angel who sees and tells, unimpeded by nicety or second thoughts.... There is also an aesthetic asset for its flavor of danger. Nothing wakes us up like menace—menace refreshes. When a poem becomes aggressive, it rouses an excitement in us, in part because we see that someone has broken their social shackles. We feel intoxicated by that outlaw freedom, and we covet it for ourselves.... Meanness clears the air of sanctimony, falsehood, and denial, of our own sentimental, ideological wishes about how things are alleged to be.... Because it does not intend to forgive nor ask forgiveness, because it does not imagine reconciliation as an end, meanness has an advantage over other kinds of discourse.... At its most radical, meanness can even have the quality of metaphysical straight-talk. Some parables of Franz Kafka, certainly, and the stories of Flannery O'Connor, offer superb examples of metaphysical meanness."

6. Show the Under-thought and Misfit Details

It's worth remembering, in our efforts to get our characters to be more unruly, we can sometimes err in the opposite direction, trying to shock readers with characters who disobey in particularly egregious ways, providing us an easy cynicism about human depravity that is just as simplistic and sentimental as work that suffers from too much niceness. I suggest that for every empathetic, generous, unadulterated pure thought and feeling, let your characters be spiteful, petty, narcissistic, and cruel. But also don't forget to go in the other direction, even with your cruelest characters. Tease out the under-thought. Look for the misfit details, the simultaneity of emotions, the redeemable in the unredeemable. Strive for density of feeling. Aim for thickness of characterization rather than consistency.

"If you have a familiar object or action to describe, you would do well not to name it, or to give it a new name, or to write it as if you're seeing it for the first time, in a state of what might be called profitable forgetting," Charles Baxter says in his essay, "On Defamiliarization." "A point of view that is off-center, a deflective point of view, may liberate the meanings of a story. As one gets older, the story of Hansel and Gretel becomes interesting only when told from the point of view of the witch. Instead of making our narrative events and our characters more colorful, we might make them thicker, more undecidable, more contradictory and unrecognizable."

7. Refuse to Judge

Anton Chekhov, in response to criticism of the lack of moral judgment in his work, said: "You abuse me for objectivity, calling it indifference to good and evil, lack of ideals and ideas, and so on. You would have me, when I describe horse-thieves, say: 'Stealing horses is an evil.' But that has been known for ages without my saying so. Let the jury judge them; it's my job simply to show what sort of people they are. I write: you are dealing with horse-thieves, so let me tell you that they are not beggars but well-fed people, that they are people of a special cult, and that horse-stealing is not simply theft but a passion. Of course it would be pleasant to combine art with a sermon, but for me personally it is extremely difficult and almost impossible, owing to the conditions of technique. You see, to depict horse-thieves in seven hundred lines I must all the time speak and think in their tone and feel in their spirit; otherwise, if I introduce subjectivity, the image becomes blurred and the story will not be as compact as all short stories ought to be. When I write, I reckon entirely upon the reader to add for himself the subjective elements that are lacking in the story."

8. Visit Trouble Upon Your Characters

Don't fall so in love with your characters that you feel skittish about applying pressure to them—to their physical selves, to their ideas of themselves, to their loved ones, to their ethical or moral values, to their spirits. John Dufresne, in *The Lie That Tells the Truth*, says that "the definition of plot is: Get your hero up a tree, throw rocks at her, throw bigger rocks at her, then get her down."

Throw rocks. Aim carefully.

9. Turn Yourself into a Character

Although it's inherently unethical to write fiction and pass it off as nonfiction, anything goes in fiction, including the fictitious use of yourself. In fact, there's a long tradition of writers who do this, and it is often the crucial identifying feature of their art. Cervantes does it in the second part of *Don Quixote*. Chaucer is one of his bumbling pilgrims in *The Canterbury Tales*. Henry Miller struts like a priapic rooster through all of his autobiographical novels. Borges routinely appears as a character in his stories, even doubling himself, which only accentuates his central themes of literary mirrors and labyrinths. (Read, for example, his famous one-page story, "Borges and I.") Philip Roth has made a career out of creating not just alter-egos such as Nathan Zuckerman but using himself fictitiously, as he does in *The Counterlife*. Tim O'Brien deliberately blurs the line between fiction and autobiography in *The Things They Carried* and *In the Lake of the Woods,* as does Kurt Vonnegut in *Slaughterhouse Five,* as does Paul Auster in many of his novels, as does Charlie Kaufman in his screenplay of *Adaptation,* where he even notoriously got screenwriting credit (and an Academy Award nomination) for his fictional twin brother.

I realize that all these examples are male, so perhaps it's a male strategy, a way of inserting the ego into the narrative, though in these instances, the version of the "I" is an intentionally false one, often designed to disarm the reader, to establish intimacy and familiarity. Such a strategy need not be gendered. Think of the work of almost every stand-up comedian; they appropriate their lives to create alternate versions of themselves for aesthetic effect.

Don't be afraid to put yourself into the books and don't be afraid to make up stuff about yourself. If your book is a "work of fiction," then that means that you, too, are a work of fiction.

10. Tone Up

Don't be so earnest. Whenever you approach a subject or characters, examine your attitude and the attitude you wish the reader to take. What is the predictable tone of your material, and how can you subvert that predictability? Can terrorism or cancer or genocide be treated comically? Can war or a devastating oil spill inspire an absurdist farce? Can your children of divorce or your orphans or your abused wives or your alcoholics or drug addicts or schleps refuse to see themselves as victims? Can they bask luxuriously in and exploit, as Shakespeare's Falstaff does, their weaknesses and misfortunes? Can you and your characters make a case against the very notion of "dysfunction"? Or can your absurdist comedy be written in a low-key, deadpan style, as many of Kafka's best tales, such as "The Metamorphosis" and "The Hunger Artist," are? "Tell the truth," Emily Dickinson famously cautioned, "but tell it slant." What she was urging, I think, is an impudent approach to tone.

Strategy, Form, Genre

Misbehaving is not just a matter of subject, characterization, or sensibility. Perhaps more importantly, disobedience is a matter of strategy, form, and genre. Too many writers, especially inexperienced ones, believe that there is a right way to do things, that there are rules of craft that writers must follow, and that technical competence matters. Mastery of technique and craft do indeed matter. No reader trusts an incompetent artist. But if the vision behind the technique is dull or predictable or formulaic—if the vision of the writer, in other words, adheres too strictly to convention—then the writer hasn't done what he or she should do. Too often writers forget that their job is primarily a subversive one. "Go forth my book," Russell Banks tells us at the end of his novel, *Continental Drift*, "and destroy the world as we know it." We must make books that are subversive. It's crucial that we as writers—not just our characters—disobey, that we create some serious structural and aesthetic mischief. What follows are some methods of artistic disobedience at the level of narrative strategy, form, and genre.

11. RE-CONCEIVE YOUR POINT OF VIEW

Point of view is the fiction writer's primary instrument, and how you use that instrument dictates the meaning of the story. I'm not talking about Keats' notion of negative capability—inhabiting a character who is very different from you. I'm talking about examining and perhaps re-conceiving the point of view you use in telling your story. Most fiction, for example, is written in either first-person or a close third-person perspective in which the voice of the narrator is almost identical to the voice of the point-of-view character.

What about a rotating first-person point of view (like Faulkner uses in *As I Lay Dying* or Barbara Kingsolver uses in *The Poisonwood Bible*), or a rotating close-third point of view (like Anne Tyler uses in *Dinner at the Homesick Restaurant* or Sena Jeter Naslund uses in *Four Spirits*)? Or what of the mixture of third and first person in most of Louise Erdrich's novels? How might these strategies help both you and the reader triangulate the complex truth or truths of your book?

What about the seldom-used first-person plural voice— the intimate community voice—that Faulkner famously employed in "A Rose for Emily" and that Joshua Ferris employs in his novel, *And Then We Came to the End?* Or what about first-person omniscience—the kind we see in Melville's *Moby-Dick* and Russell Banks' *Affliction?*

Or what about good old-fashioned omniscience—not just Virginia Woolf's kind that moves, catlike, from consciousness to consciousness, but the kind that makes grand pronouncements and judgments, that talks intimately to "the gentle reader," that acts like God and isn't afraid to look forward and backward in time and tell us what it's like in the afterlife? I'm thinking not just of the great omniscient voices of the eighteenth and nineteenth centuries—Henry Fielding, Jane Austen, George Eliot, Charles Dickens, and Leo Tolstoy—but the omniscience with an attitude of modern and contemporary writers like John Steinbeck, Joseph Heller, Toni Morrison, Gabriel Garcia Marquez, Annie Proulx, Salmon Rushdie, Larry McMurtry, Richard Russo, Jane Smiley, and Edward P. Jones. What seems to me audacious about these writers is their willingness to play God, their willingness to go against the modern inclination to tell stories in limited consciousness and instead enter freely and fully into the minds and hearts of all their characters and to have opinions about them.

Point of view is the most important decision you make as a fiction writer. Don't settle for what seems most natural or conventional or easiest. Degree of difficulty matters and is often thrilling for both writer and reader.

12. COMPRESS AND EXPAND YOUR NARRATIVE SCOPE

The standard time frame, or narrative scope, of most stories is short—a day, a week, a few months—and for most novels typically a few months or a year or two. This seems natural, given the necessity for moment-by-moment rendering of scene, for creating a vivid and continuous dream in the reader's mind. If your narrative scope is too short, you risk losing the sense of consequence or creating too much tedious detail. If your narrative scope is too long, you have to rely more on an episodic structure, as well as narrative summary and half-scene.

Though this is the conventional wisdom, is it actually valid? Why not write a novelistic story that takes place over years, even decades, as Joan Silber does in *Ideas of Heaven* and *The Size of the World* or as Annie Proulx routinely does in her Wyoming stories? Or why not write a novel or an epic about an ordinary day in the lives of very ordinary characters, as Virginia Woolf does in *Mrs. Dalloway* or James Joyce does in *Ulysses*. Or write a novel in which the primary action occurs during a very short period of time, such as the half-hour it takes a young woman to drown in Joyce Carol Oates' novel about the Chappaquiddick tragedy, *Black Water*, or the minutes of a sexual experience in Susan Minot's *Rapture*?

The art of fiction is really the art of manipulating time. How you stretch or condense time may therefore be the most disobedient, the most subversive, thing you can do.

13. Fracture Your Narrative

Every story needs a beginning, middle, and end. But you do not have to tell the story in that order. Even Aristotle advises the playwright to begin in the middle of the narrative—in *medias res*—in fact, as close to the end as possible. But you don't even have to do that. Some of the most fascinating stories, novels, and films derive their power from the authors' deliberate shattering of chronology, forcing the reader to piece the narrative together from fragments that are out of sequence.

I'm thinking, in particular, of Faulkner's *The Sound and the Fury* and *Absalom, Absalom,* of Edward P. Jones' radical use of full-blown omniscience in *The Known World*, which looks both forward and backward in time, often leaping ahead a hundred years in a single sentence. Or Charles Baxter's novel *First Light* and Harold Pinter's play *Betrayal*, both of which are told in reverse chronology. Paula Vogel's Pulitzer Prize-winning play, *How I Learned to Drive*, manipulates time to devastating effect. I'm thinking also of the fractured time sequences in films like *Citizen Kane*,

The Sweet Hereafter, Memento, Pulp Fiction, or *Babel,* or the ambitious time-shifts and embedded narratives in most of Alice Munro's stories.

Far from ruining the suspense or frustrating the reader or audience, this fracturing of narrative energizes the aesthetic experience, gives the text or film or play its urgency and power, and makes the reader an active participant in the storytelling. Or rather the "story-making." The narrative, in both senses of the word, enthralls.

14. Resurrect a Lost Form

Another way to misbehave as an author is to resurrect a lost form. Poets do this all the time. They are constantly talking about not only prosody but about resurrecting and reinventing sonnets, villanelles, sestinas, haiku, haibun, pantoums, etc. Poets understand the energy and even inherent impertinence that comes from making an old form new again. It's an act of regeneration and defamiliarization. Fiction writers can and must do this, too. Who would have thought that the parable was a viable modern form of narrative until Kafka began publishing his stories, which in turn influenced Italo Calvino and Borges and Stephen Millhauser? Or that the traditional folk or fairy tale could be the inspiration for so many of the stories and novels of Isak Dinesen, Salmon Rushdie, Gabriel Garcia Marquez, Jeannette Winterson, and Nathan

Englander? Or that a fable could be used for serious political literature until George Orwell wrote *Animal Farm*? Or that the nineteenth-century slave narrative could be transformed into something as magnificently expansive as *Beloved*? Or the quaint and obscure eighteenth-century religious tracts known as "relations" could serve as the inspiration for Russell Banks' little known but fascinating experimental novel, *The Relation of My Imprisonment*? Or that the horse opera and cattle drive narrative could be used as the template for Larry McMurtry's grand Pulitzer Prize-winning epic, *Lonesome Dove?* It's our primary job, and pleasure, as writers to discover these old forms and revitalize them—make them new again.

15. Deconstruct a Form or Genre

"… all great literature has, to some extent," John Gardner argues in *The Art of Fiction*, "a deconstructive impulse…. Throughout the history of Western civilization, we encounter a few great moments of creation—moments when the deconstructive impulse seems relatively slight—and a great many stretches of time that seem mainly devoted to taking the machinery apart and putting it together again in some new wrong way….

"Deconstruction is the practice of taking language apart, or taking works of art apart, to discover their unacknowledged inner workings. Whatever value this approach may or may not have as literary criticism, it is one of the main methods of contemporary (and sometimes ancient) fiction.... Whereas metafiction deconstructs by directly calling attention to fiction's tricks, deconstructive fiction retells the story in such a way that the old version loses credit. Shakespeare's *Hamlet* can be seen as a work of this kind. In the revenge tragedies Shakespeare's audience was familiar with, some ghost or friend or other plot-device lays on the hero the burden of avenging some crime. The genre is by nature righteous and self-confident, authoritarian: There is no doubt that vengeance is the hero's duty, and our pleasure as we watch is in seeing justice done, however painful the experience. Shakespeare's *Hamlet* deconstructs all this. Despite Horatio's certainty, we become increasingly doubtful of the ghost's authority as the play progresses, so that we become more and more concerned with Hamlet's tests of people and of himself; and even if we choose to believe that the ghost's story was true, we become increasingly unclear about whether Hamlet would be right to kill the king who usurped his father's throne—at any rate, Claudius becomes less and less the stock villain, and Hamlet, as he proceeds through the play, becomes more and more guilty himself."

This deconstructive impulse is alive and well today. Some of the most distinctive contemporary literary fiction is engaged in this type of aesthetic enterprise. Paul Auster deconstructs the detective story in his *New York Trilogy*. McMurtry and

Cormac McCarthy deconstruct the Western. E. L. Doctorow's deconstructs the gangster drama, Westerns, historical novels, political novels, novels of ideas, and coming-of-age novels. A. S. Byatt deconstructs the gothic romance in *Possession,* and John Fowles the Victorian novel in *The French Lieutenant's Woman.* Angela Carter subverts fairy tales in *The Bloody Chamber.*

Think of the genres and traditions in which your fiction operates, and then work on a story that will deconstruct that genre or tradition.

16. Pick a Fight: Intertextuality

What I encourage here is that you pick a fight or get into an argument or conversation with not just a genre or tradition, but with a specific text—a fairy tale, a myth, a story or novel by another author, living or dead. As fiction writers (or writers of other genres), we often think that our primary job is creation, that whole-cloth invention somehow distinguishes us. But there are other ways of telling a story, and many of the great writers are not great because of the originality of their stories, but because of the way they have reshaped existing stories, often with intentional malice.

"There are many ways by which one text can refer to another," David Lodge says in his collection of essays, also entitled *The Art of Fiction,* including "parody, pastiche, echo, allusion, direct quotation, structural parallelism.

Some theorists believe that intertextuality is the very condition of literature, that all texts are woven from the tissues of other texts, whether their authors know it or not."

Shakespeare, remember, "borrowed" almost all of his plots, either from history or from other writers. Homer and the Greek playwrights were retelling cultural stories that everybody already knew. There's a great contemporary tradition of this as well—the retelling of *The Odyssey* in Joyce's *Ulysses,* in Charles Frazier's *Cold Mountain,* in the Coen Brothers' *Oh, Brother, Where Art Thou?,* and in Margaret Atwood's *The Penelopiad.* Or the feminist critique of *King Lear* in Jane Smiley's *A Thousand Acres* or *The Wizard of Oz* in Gregory McGuire's *Wicked.* Or Michael Cunningham in *The Hours* and Robin Lippincott in *Mr. Dalloway* carrying on a very complex conversation with *Mrs. Dalloway.* Or Sena Jeter Naslund's epic homage to and feminist argument with Melville in *Ahab's Wife.*

Start with a familiar text and deconstruct it, do jazz riffs around the melody, pay tribute to it, and subvert it with your retelling.

17. Blur, Cross, or Elevate a Form or Genre

Sometimes, the most valuable strategy for authorial disobedience is not just re-energizing or deconstructing older forms. Sometimes we need to borrow from and elevate popular forms, what we might consider less serious forms—what Gardner calls "trash materials." Or mix forms and genres in unexpected ways.

"Though the fact is not always obvious at a glance," Gardner suggests, "when we look at works of art very close to us in time, the artist's primary unit of thought—his [or her] primary conscious or unconscious basis for selecting and organizing the details of his [or her] work—is *genre*.... When new forms arise, as they do from time to time, they rise out of one of two processes, genre-crossing or the elevation of popular culture.... Like genre-crossing, the elevation of popular or trash materials is an old and familiar form of innovation.... None of these writers, ancient or modern, sat down to write 'to express himself [or herself].' They sat down to write this kind of story or that, or to mix this form with that form, producing some new effect. Self-expression, whatever its pleasures, comes about incidentally. It also comes about inevitably."

One way, as a writer, you might do this is by poaching from the nonfiction writer and biographer's terrain. The nonfiction novel, or narrative nonfiction, are particularly ripe forms these days. Some of the most interesting work happening now is being done by first-rate novelists using subject matter that has been traditionally the domain of historians and journalists, only doing it better. I'm thinking of Don Delillo's *Libra* (Lee Oswald), Peter Carey's *The True Story of the Kelly Gang,* Sena Jeter Naslund's

Abundance (Marie Antoinette), Russell Banks' *Cloudsplitter* (the violent abolitionist John Brown), Joyce Carol Oates' *Blonde* (Marilyn Monroe), and E. L. Doctorow's *Ragtime* (a whole range of historical American figures from Emma Goldman to Henry Ford).

Or what do we make of the recent trend of writers taking popular genres and treating them with great literary panache, as we see in Cormac McCarthy's post-apocalyptic novel, *The Road;* Jonathan Lethem's detective novel, *Motherless Brooklyn;* Justin Cronin's vampire trilogy, *The Passage;* Colson Whitehead's zombie novel, *Zone One;* Max Brooks' *World War Z* (which is structured as a series of oral history interviews by survivors of a zombie outbreak); Karen Russell's brilliant mash-ups in *St. Lucy's Home for Girls Raised by Wolves* and *Vampires in the Lemon* Groves; or any one of Joyce Carol Oates' gothic horror thrillers?

How might you blur genres, or combine genres in new ways, or elevate or take seriously a popular or less serious genre?

18. Create a False Document

Of course, every piece of fiction is a false document. But there is a special kind of fiction in which the author attempts to create the illusion of the text's veracity, usually by pretending to be an editor of a manuscript written by someone else. This is Daniel Defoe's strategy in *Robinson Crusoe.* In the first of his *Tarzan* novels, Edgar Rice Burroughs writes an extended prologue in which he explains how he learned of the strange story of Lord Greystoke. Nabokov, in *Lolita*, uses an invented false editor to frame the more outlandish narrative of Humbert Humbert. In his novel, *In the Lake of the Woods,* Tim O'Brien also pretends to be a false editor, presenting all sorts of "evidence" and extended footnotes that wind up consuming the false biography by the end. E. L. Doctorow has written an eloquently persuasive essay, entitled "False Documents," in which he makes a compelling case for this kind of disobedience.

19. Indulge the Absurd Premise

Psychological realism is not the only game in town. Too many fiction writers (myself included) are overly indebted to realism. There are many other traditions of storytelling rooted in premises that are militantly anti-realistic. These stories often taken the magical world for granted and borrow from allegory, fable, fairy tale, or legend with the moral lesson implied more mysteriously and ambiguously than in those traditional forms. I'm thinking in particular of the surrealistic work of the early and middle twentieth century by visual artists, playwrights, and fiction writers such as Dali, Ionesco, Pirandello, Kafka, and Borges, but I'm also thinking of the more contemporary work of Robert Olen Butler in his collection *Tabloid Dreams,* or the magical realism of Gabriel Garcia Marquez, or the slipstream, "weird," and urban fantasy of Ursula K. Le Guin, Haruki Murakami, and China Miéville. Or the work of Louise Erdrich, Joy Harjo, N. Scott Momaday, Sherman Alexie, and Leslie Marmon Silko, rooted in American Indian mythology and storytelling. Or the nonrealistic traditions of Eastern Europe and India in Milan Kundera's and Salmon Rushdie's novels.

You might, if you want to experiment with these kinds of absurd or nonrealistic premises, start with a thought experiment: What if you took Jane Austen out on a date? What if your protagonist awoke one day to discover that she was a giant cockroach? Or you might combine unrelated spheres of experience: What would happen if a bank robbery turned into a philosophical inquiry? What if a sexual experience was subjected to the play-by-play commentary and analysis of Monday Night Football? You might think of absurd occupations: What if Vincent Van Gogh had been a dentist? What if there were hunger artists? Or professional laughers? Or you might start, as Robert Olen Butler did, with a tabloid headline: "Jealous Husband Returns in Form of Parrot."

20. STEAL AN ALTERNATIVE STRUCTURE

Stories don't have to look like stories. You can borrow a structure or form from poetry, drama, or nonfiction, or better yet, from a nonliterary source. With this strategy, your narrative is often latent or submerged in the form. In fact, in these kinds of stories, you as the writer are rebelling against conventional notions of good narrative. There's a wonderful sense of playful disobedience in alternatively structured pieces. The epistolary novel—that is, the novel told in letters—is an example of this kind of formal appropriation. As is the prose poem or the dramatic monologue.

But there can be more radical appropriations: questionnaires, multiple-choice tests, acknowledgment pages, class reunion letters, academic course descriptions, syllabi, menus, recipes, corporate memos, to-do lists, travel directions, airline itineraries, field manuals, TV guides, policies and procedures, etc. Donald Barthelme was a master of this kind of disobedience in the dozens of stories he published in *The New Yorker*. Tim O'Brien's *The Things They Carried* is comprised of stories that don't look or behave like conventional stories; they instead, are masked as how-to manuals ("How to Tell a War Story"), as lists (the title story), as autobiographical confessionals by the character known as "Tim O'Brien" ("On the Rainy River," "The Man I Killed"), or as appendices for previous pieces ("Good Form," "Notes"). Padgett Powell's *The Interrogative Mood* is a novel entirely in questions. Margaret Atwood's often-anthologized story, "Happy Endings," appears in the shape of a choose-your-own-ending multiple-choice exam.

Be on the lookout for alternative structures—they're everywhere!—and consciously think about the ways in which you might appropriate, borrow, and steal them.

These strategies for literary disobedience are, of course, meant to be suggestive rather than exhaustive. My essential argument is that great literature does not just disobey in one way; there are and perhaps should be multiple levels of disobedience, mischief, and misbehavior in any distinctive work of art. As writers, we should think of disobedience as a prerequisite of our vocation. The more ways we can misbehave, the more mischief we can make, the better—for us as writers, for the work itself, and, most importantly, for the reader.

How to begin? I suggest three quick exercises.

Think of a story, novel, poem, essay, play, or film that you love. List the ways in which the author of that text is misbehaving. Is the writer's misbehavior linked to what is distinctive or compelling about the work?

Then think of a work of your own that you are particularly proud of. How are your characters misbehaving? How are you, as an author, misbehaving? Is your misbehavior linked to what you find distinctive or compelling about your work?

Finally, think of a work of your own that you're struggling with. How can you apply one or more of these methods of misbehavior to the work in order to energize, deepen, and complicate it?

CHANNELING VOICES: ON POINT OF VIEW

Point of view is arguably the most important aspect of craft that fiction writers need to understand and, to the extent possible, master. The author's choice of point of view shapes practically every other element of the narrative: plot, characterization, voice, language, tone, imagery, and theme. In some respects, the choice is rather simple—first person or third person, or even, though less often, second person. Yet the mishandling of point of view is a frequent and significant issue in the work of not only inexperienced but sometimes seasoned fiction writers, and the issue I find myself addressing most often in my workshops and as a mentor for graduate theses. In this essay, I'll explore the significance of point of view, offer an overview of the range of point of view options, discuss why consistency when employing point of view is so crucial, examine the role of narrative distance, and suggest how point of view can be used to shape or alter meaning in a narrative.

THE SIGNIFICANCE OF POINT OF VIEW

The history of the novel—the history of fiction—is the history of point of view: from the traditional omniscient voice that we associate with the eighteenth- and nineteenth-century novelists, to the modernist breakthroughs and experiments with methods of rendering consciousness, to the postmodernist strategies that expose the essential artificiality, the hyper-self-consciousness, of inhabiting characters.

Point of view is a craft issue but also an issue irrevocably bound up with vision and sensibility. Fiction is the province of character and consciousness, and point of view is the primary artistic tool for rendering character and consciousness. Point of view determines the lens or filter through which your reader experiences the characters and the narrative. The triumph of every great novel is, I would argue, the triumph of point of view—the conception and execution and authority of the narrative voice of the story.

Most fiction writers struggle to discover the "right" point of view—a method or strategy that will best unleash the energy of the narrative and that will effectively negotiate the intersection of author, text, and reader. In reality, there is no "right" point of view; each point of view choice creates a different effect, some better than others, depending entirely upon the material and the skill of the writer. But many writers—including experienced fiction writers—are simply not aware of the range of options available to them. One goal of this essay is to suggest that range.

Third-Person Issues and Options

Why choose third person? Third person, in all its variations, is still the dominant point of view for fiction writers. The upside: this point of view allows you the greatest flexibility in terms of language and access to the consciousness of your characters. The downside: you lose some immediacy and even warmth; there is always the sense of an intermediary and an aspect of condescension because a third-person narrative voice is always removed, at least slightly, from the action—like God, as James Joyce said, behind the curtains, paring His fingernails.

Effaced (Camera Eye/Objective/Voyeur). The effaced point of view (sometimes referred to as "camera eye," "objective," or "voyeur" point of view) is the one most associated with minimalist fiction and the one that steals most blatantly from the art of playwriting. In a purely effaced point of view, the authorial voice does not enter the consciousness of any character. What we learn about the characters is revealed to us, as in a film or play, through dialogue, action, and gesture. Those who favor this point of view—typically writers drawn to plays or to the radically minimalist tradition—argue that this method allows or forces the reader to participate more fully in creating the drama and refer to signature stories such as Ernest Hemingway's

"Hills Like White Elephants," Raymond Carver's "Popular Mechanics," Philip Roth's novel *Deception,* or some of the dialogue-driven sudden fiction of Amy Hempel. The primary problem with this point of view is that it unnecessarily limits the available tools for storytelling or actually abdicates more sophisticated methods of rendering consciousness. It is often the default point of view for fiction writers who have not figured out effective methods for rendering interiority.

Limited Omniscience (or Close Third/Central Intelligence). A limited-omniscience or "close third" technique involves the writer rigorously filtering the narrative through the consciousness of one character. That focal character's thoughts, memories, perceptions, and sensory experiences are the lens through which the reader experiences the story. Most fiction writers employ this strategy. A more liberal use of this point of view allows the writer to both render internally the experience of the focal character and to describe that character externally as well. The great advantage of this point of view is that it allows deep access to the protagonist, while giving the writer a more flexible range of language with which to work, marrying the character's way of thinking and talking with the writer's greater facility and eloquence with language rhythms, thoughts, and feelings. Unlike first-person point of view—which often necessitates a retrospective perspective and a more explicit rationale for the telling of the story—limited omniscience plunges us into the character's internal experience without the self-consciousness and performative ventriloquism of first-person narration. I used this method for my novel, *The Girl from Charnelle,* after writing full drafts in first person and omniscient point of view. Joyce Carol Oates' famous and much-anthologized "Where Are You Going, Where Have You Been?" is a particularly powerful example of limited omniscience, taking us deeply inside the protagonist Connie's interior perceptions, in a highly disciplined way, as she undergoes a traumatic event.

Rotating Limited Omniscience. Most novels and stories that we think of as omniscient can be more accurately described as "rotating limited omniscient." That is, each chapter (or section of the story) rotates in terms of its access to two or more characters. For example, Mary may be the focal character in chapter one, John in chapter two, Gabriel in chapter three, Mary in four, and so on. This strategy allows for the kind of panoramic breadth that is the great allure of omniscience, while still providing the depth and clarity of focus of limited omniscience. Joyce Carol Oates' *You Must Remember This,* Anne Tyler's *Dinner at the Homesick Restaurant,* Pete Dexter's *Paris Trout,* T. C. Boyle's great story "Balto," John Updike's *Rabbit Angstrom* novels, and John Pipkin's wonderful novel about a young

Henry David Thoreau, *Woodsburner,* are all examples of this strategy.

Neutral Omniscience. Unlike the rotating limited omniscience, which more neatly and clearly demarcates the point-of-view character, often using chapter or space breaks to indicate a shift in perspective, the neutral (or standard) omniscience moves, cat-like, in and out of the consciousness of the characters, often without clearly delineated transitions. While this point of view is much more flexible, the author renders the story *through* the characters in a highly disciplined way, without commentary or explicit judgment. Joseph Conrad and Henry James preferred this method of disciplined "rendering" of character. John Steinbeck uses this method throughout most of *The Grapes of Wrath,* especially the longer chapters devoted to the Joad family. This is also Virginia Woolf's favored method; in fact, she perfected, if not invented it. It's the voice, to a certain extent, of Flannery O'Connor, in classic stories like "A Good Man Is Hard to Find" and "Good Country People." It, in fact, is the preferred method of most writers who wish to take us into and out of many characters' minds, move us backward and forward in time, but do so primarily through deep immersion in the characters' consciousnesses without obtrusive authorial presence.

Chatty Omniscience (or Omniscience with an Attitude). This is the voice we more naturally associate with classic literature, a point of view in which the omniscient voice intrudes and comments on the action and characters. With this point of view, the narrative voice emerges as a character—the raconteur, the performative storyteller. We fall in love with that voice, that narrative strategy, as much if not more than we do with the characters. This is the voice we most often associate with classic eighteenth- and nineteenth-century novelists such as Jane Austen (all of her novels), Henry Fielding (*Tom Jones*), Victor Hugo (*Les Misérables*), Leo Tolstoy (*War and Peace, The Death of Ivan Ilyich, Anna Karenina*), George Eliot (*Middlemarch*), Charles Dickens (*A Tale of Two Cities, Hard Times,* and *Bleak House*), as well as modern and contemporary writers such as Steinbeck (*Cannery Row*), Toni Morrison (*Beloved*), E. L. Doctorow (*The March*), John Irving (*The World According to Garp*), Edward P. Jones (*The Known World*), and Annie Proulx (*Close Range, The Shipping News*), and almost anything by Gabriel Garcia Marquez. This is the point of view of God, a voice that knows, as God does, past, present, and future. It's also the point of view of most traditional forms of fiction: the fairy tale, the allegory, the epic poem. Think "Once upon a time…." There is something both dignified and unrestrained about this strategy, and it is perhaps the most audacious point of view, requiring enormous authority or chutzpah on the part of the writer.

First-Person Issues and Options

Why choose first-person point of view? The great advantage of first person is that it mimics the way we really tell stories in our lives—in families, among friends, in everyday discourse. There is greater immediacy and warmth in a first-person narration because a human being always resides behind that "I"—or at least a sentient presence, if you're writing about monsters, hobgoblins, or androids. Robert Olen Butler has argued, in *From Where You Dream,* that first person is the only point of view that captures the residue of human yearning, which for him is central to the art of fiction.

The disadvantage of first person is that, as a writer, you are constricted by the voice of the narrator or narrators you choose, and that limitation dictates language, syntax, perspective, everything. It can be a wearying experience for both a writer and a reader to be stuck inside a single first-person voice for four hundred pages.

There are, however, political and philosophical reasons for using first person. If one of your aims as a writer is to give voice to the voiceless, to help us listen to the stories of the marginalized, then letting your characters tell their own stories, in their own vernacular poetry, is not just a craft choice; it's a political act. Other writers prefer first person over, say, omniscience, because they fundamentally don't believe in a method that assumes a god-like stance or suggests one kind of truth. In a post-postmodern world, truth is always subjective, never objective.

Once you've chosen a first-person strategy, perhaps your most significant decision is whether your narrator is writing or talking to the reader. Is this a consciously constructed literary document that operates as a fictional memoir, or is it a spoken text that operates as a soliloquy or monologue? One key aspect of this dichotomy concerns verb tense. Characters who talk often do so in present tense, as if the narrative is unfolding as an interior monologue. Characters who are consciously composing a text often do so in past tense, and the point in time from which the narrative is being written—what I call the "fixed point in the retrospective narration"—is made explicit. Most first-person narrators in Dickens are memoirists; most first-person narrators in Faulkner are talkers. Huck Finn and Holden Caulfield are talkers. Ishmael in *Moby-Dick,* Jane in *Jane Eyre,* Nick Carraway in *The Great Gatsby,* Humbert Humbert in Nabokov's *Lolita,* Ginny in Jane Smiley's *A Thousand Acres,* Una in Sena Jeter Naslund's *Ahab's Wife,* and Jack Burden in Robert Penn Warren's *All the King's Men* are memoirists.

Another crucial question for first-person narration involves reliability. Reliability and unreliability are not evaluative or derogatory terms; they are descriptive terms. To a greater or lesser degree, every first-person narrator is unreliable because, as humans, we have limited access to and understanding of any kind of objective truth. Reliable narrators are those whose reportage and insights about characters and events we generally trust. With an unreliable narrator, the author has intentionally leveraged the narrator's untrustworthiness as a reporter and interpreter of events to the advantage of the story; in fact, that gap often *is* the story. All child narrators (not retrospective narrators looking back on childhood) are, by definition, unreliable. Huck Finn, Holden Caulfield, the narrator of Ford Maddox Ford's *The Good Soldier,* the butler in Kazuo Ishiguro's *Remains of the Day,* and most Poe, Faulkner, and Louise Erdrich narrators are studies in unreliable narration. Dickens' David Copperfield and Pip, Melville's Ishmael, Fitzgerald's Nick Carraway, Penn Warren's Jack Burden, Harper Lee's Scout, the narrator of James Baldwin's "Sonny's Blues," Frank Bascombe of Richard Ford's Bascombe Trilogy are, by and large, reliable narrators. In general, the more removed in time the narrator is from the events that he or she is telling, the greater the reliability.

In most cases, a first-person narrator is, by default, the protagonist of the narrative because the narrator is the central interpreting consciousness of fiction. But narrators may be directly or indirectly involved in the action. Directly involved narrators are those who are telling significant events in their lives, and their stories tend to be narratives of identity and transformation (e.g., Dickens' *David Copperfield* and *Great Expectations,* Naslund's *Ahab's Wife,* Saul Bellow's *The Adventures of Augie March,* Ralph Ellison's *Invisible Man*), narratives of accusation (e.g., most narratives that have whistle-blowing or the perspective of victims at their center), or narratives of confession or vindication (e.g., Smiley's *A Thousand Acres,* Roth's *Portnoy's Complaint,* Tim O'Brien's "On the Rainy River").

Indirectly involved narrators are those who serve as interpreters and sense-makers but who are not central to the action of the narrative and who may not be considered (or do not consider themselves) the protagonists. These narrators may act as editors (Daniel Defoe's persona in *Robinson Crusoe,* the editor character in *Lolita,* Tim O'Brien's author-editor in *In the Lake of the Woods*), as reporters or biographers (the narrator Rolph of *Affliction,* Nathan Zuckerman in Roth's *American Pastoral*), or as witnesses or allies of the protagonist (Ishmael, Nick Carraway, Jack Burden, the narrator of Melville's "Bartleby, the Scrivener").

Rotating First Person. Like rotating limited omniscience, rotating first person splits the narrative focus among several characters. The meaning of the narrative often arises from the interplay and triangulation of voices. This strategy often feels like a *tour de force,* an act of ventriloquism in which the meaning derives from the variety of voices. Faulkner's *As I Lay Dying* is perhaps the most famous example. Barbara Kingsolver's *The Poisonwood Bible* is one of the best contemporary examples, along with Larry McMurtry's *Leaving Cheyenne,* Lee Martin's *The Bright Forever,* Louise Erdrich's *Tracks,* Russell Banks's *The Sweet Hereafter,* as well as most of the work of the great short story cyclist, Joan Silber (*Ideas of Heaven, The Size of the World, Fools, Improvement*).

First-Person Plural. Seldom-used, this communal voice often is striking in terms of creating the effect of a Greek chorus. Faulkner's "A Rose for Emily" is the most frequently cited example. Karen Russell uses this point of view in the first three quarters of her celebrated story, "St. Lucy's Home for Girls Raised by Wolves." Joshua Ferris' novel, *Then We Came to the End,* is an excellent book-length example.

First-Person Omniscience. In this point of view, the narrator assumes the ability to render the consciousness of other characters as an omniscient narrator would do. I'm not talking about a chatty omniscient narrator, who is often a persona of the writer, but rather a character in the narrative who imagines the inner lives of others and events he or she has not witnessed. Sometimes the narrator offers a rationale for the method—exhaustive research, imaginative license, intuition—but sometimes not. Examples: Ishmael in much of Melville's *Moby-Dick* and Rolph in Russell Banks' *Affliction*. In addition, E. L. Doctorow's *Ragtime* and Ian McEwan's *Atonement* are brilliant examples of secret first-person narratives posing, until the end of the books, as omnisciently told novels.

Second-Person Issues

Why choose second-person point of view? This point of view is one of the riskier options because it can seem gimmicky, though there are many natural ways in which we invoke a "you" in a narrative. It can also be leveraged to wonderful effect—most often a comic effect—when used as a substitute for first person.

You, Dear Reader. Often the "you" of a narrative is literally the reader and can be used by either a third-person narrator or a first-person narrator as a way of "breaking frame," of directly addressing the reader. Many eighteenth- and nineteenth-century writers used this strategy, most notably Henry Fielding in *Tom Jones*. John Fowles, in his postmodern version of a Victorian novel, *The French Lieutenant's Woman*, employs this frame-breaking technique.

Dramatic Monologues. When a character addresses a "you" in scene, and that "you" is clearly a character who is simply not speaking, then we have a dramatic monologue—a form that has its origins in drama and poetry. The reader (or audience) acts as eavesdropper for the one-sided conversation. Andrew Marvell's "To His Coy Mistress" and Robert Browning's "My Last Duchess" are two of the most famous poetic examples of this form. My collection of poems, *Lost Soliloquies,* contains several dramatic monologues. Jane Martin's *Talking With* and Heather Raffo's *9 Parts of Desire* are plays in the form of dramatic monologues. Jamaica Kincaid's "Girl" and Philip Roth's *Portnoy's Complaint* are notable examples in fiction.

Epistles. A narrative consisting of letters—either one-sided letters or exchanged letters—is another natural way to tell stories using second person. As in dramatic monologues, there is an implied character who is the "you." Samuel Richardson in *Clarissa* turned this epistolary mode into literature and began a tradition that has persisted into the age of email, Instagram, Facebook, and Twitter. Alice Walker's *The Color Purple,* Diane Smith's *Letters from Yellowstone,* and Julie Schumacher's *Dear Committee Members* are excellent contemporary examples of epistolary narratives.

Instructions, Self-Help Manuals, Directions, Guidebooks. Narratives that borrow these types of non-literary forms of communication also tap into a second-person voice that feels organic to our real lives, if not our normal mode of storytelling. Lorrie Moore's *Self-Help* is probably the best example of this.

You as "Ashamed I." Pam Houston argues that "you," when used as a replacement for "I," is a method of exposing what she calls the "ashamed I." In this kind of narrative, the "you" is particularized in great detail and clearly not a reference to the reader or another character. Jay McInerney's *Bright Lights, Big City* is a famous contemporary book-length example, as are many of Pam Houston's own stories published in *Cowboys Are My Weakness,* such as "How to Talk to a Hunter." Often, as this last example by Houston and many of Lorrie Moore's *Self-Help* stories suggest, the "ashamed I" overlaps with the instruction/self-help-manual use of second person. "One of the interesting effects of the second person," Joseph M. Schuster points out, "is that it can create a clear and often uncomfortable tension for the reader, since it also can seem to be a mirror in which we are looking at ourselves, or being invited to look at ourselves in a defamiliarized way. In Frederick Barthleme's second-person story, 'Shop Girls,' for example, the protagonist seems frozen, unable to act in a way that makes the reader uncomfortable, since he seems to suggest that we are the ones unable to act. The story also creates tension because the character is a kind of voyeur, spying on women who work in a department store, trying to avoid getting caught staring but caught nonetheless."

Narrative (or Psychic) Distance

Narrative distance (often referred to as psychic distance) in point of view refers to how shallowly or how deeply the narrative voice, typically in third person, enters the consciousness of the character.

John Gardner, in *The Art of Fiction,* was one of the first novelists to pay close attention to the significance of narrative/psychic distance in point of view. "By psychic distance," he writes, "we mean the distance the reader feels between himself and the events of the stories. Compare the following examples, the first meant to establish great psychic distance, the next meant to establish slightly less, and so on until in the last example, psychic distance, theoretically at least, is nil. '(1) It was winter of 1853. A large man stepped out of a doorway. (2) Henry J. Warburton had never much cared for snowstorms. (3) Henry hated snowstorms. (4) God, how he hated these damn snowstorms. (5) Snow. Under your collar, down inside your shoes, freezing and plugging up your miserable soul.' When psychic distance is great, we look at the scene as if from far away—our usual position in the traditional tale, remote in time and space, formal in presentations (example 1 above would appear only in a tale); as distance grows shorter—as the camera dollies in, if you will—we approach the normal ground of the yarn (2 and 3) and short story or realist novel (2 through 5). In good fiction, shifts in psychic distance are carefully controlled. At the beginning of the story, in the usual case, we find the writer using either long or medium shots. He moves in a little for scenes of high intensity, draws back for transitions, moves in still closer for the story's climax."

Interior Monologue and Stream of Consciousness. Acclaimed British novelist, David Lodge, who was also a renowned narrative theorist and literary critic, articulates two other crucial aspects of point of view in his version of *The Art of Fiction*. "There are two staple techniques for representing consciousness in prose fiction," he says. "The first method is interior monologue, in which the grammatical subject of the discourse is an 'I,' and we, as it were, overhear the character verbalizing his or her thoughts, as they occur. We become acquainted with the principal characters not by being told about them, but by sharing their most intimate thoughts, represented as silent, spontaneous, unceasing streams of consciousness. For the reader, it's rather like wearing earphones plugged into someone's brain, and monitoring an endless tape-recording of the subject's impressions, reflections, questions, memories and fantasies, as they are triggered by physical sensations or the association of ideas…. Interior monologue is indeed a very difficult technique to use successfully, all too apt to impose a painfully slow pace on the narrative and to bore the reader with a plethora of detail."

Free Indirect Style. "The other method," David Lodge continues, "is called free indirect style, and goes back at least as far as Jane Austen, but was employed with ever-increasing scope and virtuosity by modern novelists like Virginia Woolf. It renders thought as reported speech (in the third person, past tense) but keeps to the kind of vocabulary that is appropriate to the character, and deletes some of the tags, like 'she thought,' 'she wondered,' 'she asked herself,' etc. This gives the illusion of intimate access to a character's mind, but without totally surrendering authorial participation in the discourse."

The Fixed Point in Retrospective Narration. In any first-person, past-tense narration, there are two characters—the narrator who went through the events and the narrator who is now telling the story (and presumably trying to make some sense) of those events. That dual vision is the great advantage and pleasure of writing and reading such narratives. The fixed point in the retrospective narration is the point in time from which a first-person narrative is being written. Is the narrative being told from a one-day remove, a one-year remove, or a twenty-year remove? This temporal distance matters tremendously, as it shapes the voice and dictates the reliability and perspective of the narrator. As a writer, you must figure out that fixed point early in the process, even if it does not become an explicit aspect of the narrative. You, as a writer, must know it.

PROBLEMS OF EXECUTION
Consistency of Perspective. "One of the commonest signs of a lazy or inexperienced writer of fiction is inconsistency in handling point of view," David Lodge argues. "A story—let us say it is the story of John, leaving home for the first time

to go to University, as perceived by John—John packing his bag, taking a last look round his bedroom, saying goodbye to his parents—and suddenly, for just a couple of sentences, we are told what his mother is thinking about the event, merely because it seemed to the writer an interesting bit of information to put in at that point; after which the narrative carries on from John's point of view. Of course, there is no rule or regulation that says a novel may not shift its point of view whenever the writer chooses; but if it is not done according to some aesthetic plan or principle, the reader's involvement, the reader's 'production' of the meaning of the text, will be disturbed. We may wonder, consciously or subliminally, why, if we have been told what John's mother was thinking at one point in the scene, we haven't been given the same access to her mind at other moments. The mother, who was up to that point an object of John's perception, has suddenly become a subject in her own right, but an incompletely realized one. And, if we are given access to the mother's point of view, why not the father's too?"

Consistency in Psychic Distance. "A piece of fiction containing sudden and inexplicable shifts in psychic distance looks amateur and tends to drive the reader away," Gardner asserts. "For instance: 'Mary Borden hated woodpeckers. Lord, she thought, they'll drive me crazy! The young woman had never known any personally, but Mary knew what she liked.' Clumsy writing of this kind cannot help distracting the reader from the dream and thus ruining or seriously impairing the fiction."

Unclear Fixed Point. In first-person narratives, the most frequent mistake is the writer's failure to identify the point in time from which the narrator is telling his or her story, especially a story about childhood. In some cases, as in the opening pages of Alice Munro's great story, "Miles City, Montana," an unclear fixed point can be used intentionally. "My father came across the field carrying the body of the boy who had been drowned," the narrator says, and then the story leaps ahead twenty years in the next scene. The time-bending is intentional in that story (as it is in so many of Munro's first-person narratives), especially when her narrator circles back to the original story of a drowned child at the end. But most writers do not possess Munro's mastery, and the result often is a narrative voice that sounds schizophrenic, sometimes falling into a kind of baby talk, with the diction and lack of perspective or interiority of a young child juxtaposed clumsily against the eloquence and wisdom of a much older narrator looking back with the perspective and irony of time.

Writers and Critics on Point of View

Henry James. In his prefaces to his novels, published late in his life, James provides a comprehensive examination by a writer of the fictional process and the conscious deployment of literary technique. His major breakthrough was in what he called a "scenic method," or what we now think of as central intelligence, close third, or limited omniscience—a method that grants the writer deep access to the consciousness of the characters without abdicating the writer's more objective and eloquent control over language and voice. James was determined, in both his own fiction and his critical work, to make fiction a high art rather than what he called "the loose baggy monsters" written by Victorian novelists such as Dickens and Thackery. Often what he objected to most in those writers was their expansive or, to James' mind, sloppy deployment of point of view.

Percy Lubbock, *The Craft of Fiction*. This is one of the first detailed modernist discussions of the technique of fiction. Using James as his exemplary model, Lubbock makes an extended case for point of view as the primary instrument of the art of fiction. He also argues for a restricted and masterful execution of the scenic method and central intelligence point of view.

E. M. Forster, *Aspects of the Novel*. In this landmark series of lectures, Forster, author of early twentieth-century classics such *A Passage to India* and *A Room with a View*, examines different aspects of the novel. His approach to point of view is in sharp contrast to that of Lubbock and James. He argues that a writer shouldn't be slavish to any technique, including point of view. He says the great writers—Dickens, in particular—are great precisely because they have the ability to "bounce" the reader around from consciousness to consciousness without the reader minding.

Mark Schorer, "Technique as Discovery." In this landmark 1948 essay, first published in *The Hudson Review*, Schorer argues that technique (which he interprets essentially as point of view) is the primary method by which meaning is made in a narrative. Here's an excerpt: "When we speak of technique, we speak of nearly everything. For technique is the means by which the writer's experience, which is his subject matter, compels him to attend to it; technique is the only means he has of discovering, exploring, developing his subject, of conveying its meaning, and, finally of evaluating it. And surely it follows that certain techniques [by which he again primarily means point of view] are sharper tools than others, and will discover more; that the writer capable of the most exacting technical scrutiny of his subject matter will produce works with the most satisfying content, works with thickness and resonance, works which reverberate, works with maximum meaning."

John Gardner, *The Art of Fiction*. This is still one of the most influential books on the craft and art of fiction. He spends more time talking about genre and form than point of view. But his major contribution to the discussion of point of view concerns what he calls "psychic distance."

Wayne C. Booth, "Types of Narration" in *The Rhetoric of Fiction*. Among literary critics who don't write fiction themselves, Booth has a great deal to say to fiction writers about both the theory and practice of fiction. His theory involves an examination of point of view in terms of dramatized and un-dramatized narrators, observers and narrator-agents, scene and summary, commentary, self-conscious narrators, privilege, inside views, and variations of distance.

David Lodge, *The Art of Fiction* and *The Consciousness of the Novel*. In *The Art of Fiction,* Lodge provides a very helpful and accessible overview and examples of different narrative techniques, with considerable time spent on various strategies of point of view. His more theoretically dense but still accessible *The Consciousness of the Novel* makes a compelling case for the innovation of "free indirect" point of view being the major breakthrough in the evolution of the novel.

Robert Olen Butler, *From Where You Dream*. Butler, the Pulitzer Prize-winning short story writer and novelist, lays out a persuasive case for a more organic approach to fiction writing that is inspired by Stanislavski's approach to acting—what later became the American "method" style of acting. In terms of his own evolution as a writer, Butler claimed at one point that all of his new fiction would be in first person, even though most of his early novels were third person. (He has since written in third person. Writers shouldn't be held accountable for their promises.) He believes, as I mentioned earlier, that fiction is the "art of yearning," and that first person is the most potent instrument for expressing that yearning. His chapter in *From Where You Dream,* entitled "The Cinema of the Mind," in which he compares cinematic technique to fictional technique, is a perceptive contribution to the discussion of the significance of point of view as the primary tool for the fiction writer.

Debra Spark, "Stand Back" in *Curious Attractions.* An illuminating essay about the advantages and uses of omniscience and a clear, effective explanation of what Gardner meant by psychic (or narrative) distance. She also speaks eloquently about what she calls the narrator as omniscient storyteller.

Richard Russo, "On Omniscience" in *The Destiny Thief: Essays on Writers, Writing and Life.* Russo discusses the practicalities of using omniscient point of view, a technique that he has clearly mastered, most notably in his Pulitzer Prize-winning epic, *Empire Falls,* as well as the comic duo of novels, *Nobody's Fool* and *Everybody's Fool.*

Robert Boswell, "In Defense of Omniscience" in *The Half-Known World: On Writing Fiction.* An excellent essay in an excellent collection of essays, in which Boswell makes a complex case for not only how to handle omniscient point of view but why it is an invaluable narrative strategy.

James Wood, *How Fiction Works*. One of the most nuanced discussions of point of view, especially the free indirect style, by *The New Yorker* critic and husband of acclaimed novelist Claire Messud.

Jane Smiley, *13 Ways of Looking at the Novel*. One of my favorite books on the art of fiction by a practitioner of the art. She doesn't devote any single chapter to point of view, but she writes insightfully and comprehensively about the art and evolution of the novel. Her chapters on "The Psychology of the Novel" relate directly to issues of point of view.

DESCRIBE, PRAISE, QUESTION: WORKSHOP AS GIFT COMMUNITY

At its best, a creative writing workshop serves as an aesthetic laboratory, clarifying what is strongest and weakest about each work-in-progress. One of the central problems with the traditional workshop process, however, is that it often operates as a fault-finding mechanism. It tends to reduce the level of discourse to praise and blame: *This is what we liked; this is what we want you to fix.* As both teachers and students, we sometimes forget that the purpose of workshop—in fact, the primary task of criticism—is not necessarily to help the writer "fix" the story, poem, essay, or script, but rather to describe, appreciate, and illuminate it as accurately, generously, and persuasively as we can, not only for the writer's benefit but for the benefit of the entire group. The workshop should ideally sharpen your ability to read, understand, and explicate *any* work, whether the ill-conceived manuscript of a beginning writer or the masterpiece of a Nobel laureate.

The best kind of workshop is characterized, I believe, by the following conditions. The workshop should offer a writer the benefit of having the focused and scrupulous attention of a community of readers, some more discriminating than others. The workshop helps you clarify your vision and fine-tune your stories, poems, scripts, essays, and novels. As a responder to other work, the workshop process gives you the opportunity to practice reading carefully and rigorously, and to problem-solve not only your own work but the works-in-progress of others—writing that may be very different from yours in terms of sensibility, style, and strategy. For the group, the workshop provides a reliable method by which each member discovers his or her own artistic goals and vision and more clearly begins to understand and articulate the goals and vision of others. It can be, as anyone who has been a creative writing student or teacher knows full well, a powerful experience.

The worst kind of workshop is often characterized by these conditions: for the writer, it can be a dreadful and dehumanizing event that short-circuits confidence and makes you less willing to take risks. You can wind up more confused than ever about the vision and execution of the work and will attempt to revise in order to please the majority. For the responder, it can be a baffling enterprise in which you feel ill-equipped to critique work that either does not interest you or that you do not understand. Your response becomes an inventory of your own half-articulated tastes, biases, and moods rather than disciplined practice in careful reading. There is often the palpable assumption, in a poor workshop, that the group is the reservoir of wisdom and an enforcer of taste—that the workshop serves as a jury empaneled to pass judgment on the texts before it. Each writer takes a turn as the defendant, offering his or her manuscript as fraught testimony, dreading the verdict.

Most workshops, of course, occupy a gray zone between these two extremes. There are always a few people who genuinely understand your work and whose criticism you come to value. Most workshops try to balance praise with criticism so that the work is lauded for its strengths and taken to task for its weaknesses. And the opportunity to have a group of smart and committed writers read your work closely is, overall, an energizing and motivating experience, if for no other reason than fear: you do not want to embarrass yourself by presenting sloppy work to people you respect and admire.

I believe the key to a healthy and successful workshop is the level and quality of preparation that students and teachers, as workshop participants, put into their written critiques—and the implications of that preparation. More than thirty years of workshop experience have shown me that most apprentice writers aren't very adept at dealing with the works-in-progress of others. They assume that their job is to diagnose what's wrong with the manuscripts they're examining. They often assume, in fact, that there *is* something wrong, and they feel guilty if they cannot point out mistakes or make any substantive suggestions for revision. Or they feel emboldened by the license of workshop to eviscerate the poem, story, essay, or script. Their analyses, when extensive, are often subject to aesthetic or emotional whims. Not a lot of clear-headed, rigorous investigation of the manuscript occurs.

The primary problem, I believe, is that the individual critiques are frequently *responder-centered* rather than *text-centered*, and prescriptive rather than descriptive.

What do I mean by these distinctions? Let me provide an extended example of the difference between a prescriptive responder-centered critique and a descriptive text-centered critique. Below is a very short story by Raymond Carver, originally published as "Popular Mechanics," and later republished as "Little Things," which for my purposes here I'll use as the workshop story.

Popular Mechanics

Early that day the weather turned and the snow was melting into dirty water. Streaks of it ran down from the little shoulder-high window that faced the back yard. Cars slushed by on the street outside, where it was getting dark. But it was getting dark on the inside too.

He was in the bedroom pushing clothes into a suitcase when she came to the door.

I'm glad you're leaving! I'm glad you're leaving, she said. Do you hear?

He kept putting his thing into the suitcase.

Son of a bitch! I'm so glad you're leaving! She began to cry. You can't even look at me in the face, can you?

Then she noticed the baby's picture on the bed and picked it up.

He looked at her and she wiped her eyes and stared at him before turning and going back to the living room.

She stood in the doorway of the little kitchen, holding the baby.

I want the baby, he said.

Are you crazy?

No, but I want the baby. I'll get someone to come by for his things.

You're not touching the baby, she said.

The baby had begun to cry and she uncovered the blanket from around his head.

Oh, oh, she said, looking at the baby.

He moved toward her.

For God's sake! she said. She took a step back into the kitchen.

I want the baby.

Get out of here!

She turned and tried to hold the baby over in a corner behind the stove.

But he came up. He reached across the stove and tightened his hands on the baby.

Let go of him, he said.

Get away, get away! she cried.

The baby was red-faced and screaming. In the scuffle they knocked down a flowerpot that hung behind the stove.

He crowded her into the wall then, trying to break her grip. He held on to the baby and pushed with all his weight.

Let go of him, he said.

Don't, she said. You're hurting the baby, she said.

I'm not hurting the baby, he said.

The kitchen window gave no light. In the near-dark he worked on her fisted fingers with one hand and with the other hand he gripped the screaming baby up under an arm near the shoulder.

She felt her fingers being forced open. She felt the baby going from her.

No! she screamed just as her hands came loose.

She would have it, this baby. She grabbed for the baby's other arm. She caught the baby around the wrist and leaned back.

But he would not let go. He felt the baby slipping out of his hands and he pulled back very hard.

In this manner, the issue was decided.

A Responder-Centered Critique

Here is an example of a responder-centered critique of this story, as it might be written if the story had been submitted to an undergraduate or graduate workshop.

Hey Big Ray—

This is some scary shit, man. I love all that "dirty water" imagery at the beginning and the way "it was getting dark on the inside too." Very cinematic, but also *très* symbolic. (But is it perhaps too symbolic? Just asking.) The wife is quite the harridan, don't you think? All that screeching about being so glad he's leaving, so glad he's leaving, when of course she's not glad at all. You really made me feel her bitchery.

I'm sort of baffled by how little the story's fleshed out. This isn't even five hundred words. I thought we berated you thoroughly last workshop on this "leaving too much out" business. There aren't even any quotation marks. I know your due date for workshop was the day after we were at Lyzzard's until the wee hours of the old a.m. If I recall clearly (always a shaky assumption), that was the night you broke the pool cue across that burly biker's head. (Was I dreaming, or did he have a horse tattooed on his skull?) Anyway, I wonder if you rushed this to meet the deadline—it has the feel of a hangover. (Been there, done that.)

So, back to the brevity of this piece. The characters don't even have names! Just a generic wife, generic husband, generic baby. And we never get inside their heads. Where's the interiority, man? Why is he leaving? Shouldn't we at least know that much?

Where's the backstory? It's like you just pointed the camera at them. Can't we get inside one of the characters' heads or feelings? And because I'm not inside anyone's consciousness, it's hard to feel any empathy or sympathy for this couple—except perhaps for that poor armless baby. (Sounds like a sick joke, Big Ray.) At least make it first person from the man's or woman's perspective; that way I'd have someone to root for. And, quite frankly, you're better at first person than third.

Also, you have to lay off the Hemingway stories for a while! I kept thinking that this was what happened to the couple in "Hills Like White Elephants" if they decided to have the kid after all.

I longed for the blind man from that last story. Where's the shared doobie? Where are the cathedrals, man?

"In this matter, the issue was decided." Be truthful: Have you really earned that ending? Seems to me that not much has been decided, has it? Is this another attempt at irony? Irony just does not become you, Big Ray. You are all about earnestness. And "Popular Mechanics"—where did that come from? I don't see anything popular or mechanical in this story. I think you've been sucking on one too many burnt roaches, brother. (Been there, done that.)

Suggestion alert: What about "Little Things" as your title, especially if you're aiming for irony? Little things do mean a lot.

Overall, though, I really like this draft. Scary shit—with a lot of potential. (Should I be worried about you? Should I call Social Services?) I just wish you'd scratch below the surface and get to those thorny marital dynamics you know so much about.

Remember: I only criticize because I love. You know you rock.

See you at happy hour. 4:15, Lyzzard's. You owe me a margarita because my response is longer than your story, man. (Who's doing the work here?) Stay away from the pool cues and the tattooed horses. At least until I get there.

—Kenardo

To its credit, such a response does have energy and attempts to express the emotional effect of the piece on this reader: "scary shit," "you really made me feel her bitchery." It's also personal, avoiding the pedantic tone of a formal literary analysis. There is some level of sophisticated insight, raising questions about not just the intentions of the piece but the narrative strategies and craft choices. And it offers potentially useful suggestions.

What's problematic about this responder-centered critique? The primary issue for me is that familiarity here breeds a patronizing contempt, one of the major challenges of resident undergraduate and graduate programs, in which the same students analyze each other's work over a two-to-four-year period. The response is deeply rooted in the responder's preferences and prejudices. Most of the suggestions do not emerge from a rigorous attempt to understand and appreciate the story on its own terms. The response relies instead on quasi-authoritative, sweeping generalizations about Big Ray's strengths (first person, thorny marital dynamics) and his weaknesses (irony, leaving out the interiority, laziness). It is, in short, prescriptive without earning the right to be so.

If the responses that I sometimes received as a student and the responses that my own students sometimes write for each other are any indication, such a critique is more common than we would like to acknowledge. Whatever its charms (I turned this critique into a poem, included in my collection, *Lost Soliloquies*), there's something pernicious about this kind of response. It is more about the responder than the writer and the piece, the responder wanting to show how smart and clever he is. It also has the potential to undermine what may be most unique about a writer's work—and to discourage the writer from taking thematic, formal, and stylistic risks.

Descriptive Questions: Who, What, Where, When, Why, and How?

Over the years, I have given workshop process a great deal of both practical and philosophical thought, and I have had the opportunity to experiment with and develop other models for workshop that can open up possibilities for richer discussions and critiques. The method that has been most successful for me is one that prioritizes description and analysis, rooted in the close analysis I learned in my literature training. Let me describe that method and then apply it to "Popular Mechanics."

Below is a series of adapted journalistic questions that I've been using for several years to help guide my students' responses to one another.

Who? (Characterization). Who are the characters in the story? Who is the protagonist? Does the protagonist move the action? Is this protagonist moved by the action, and, if so, in what way? What does the protagonist yearn for and fear? What secret is the protagonist harboring or investigating? Who are the secondary, or fixed, characters in the story? What purpose do they serve?

What? (Plot/Conflict). What happens? What is the plot? What are the sources of conflict or tension? What are the scenes, and what is summarized?

Where? (Setting). Where does the story take place? Is setting or environment integral to the meaning of the story? How so?

When? (Time/Temporal Scope). When does the story take place? Is the era, season, day, or time crucial to the meaning of the story? What is the temporal scope of the story? How much time is covered in the narrative? If the story is told in first person, is there a clearly articulated temporal distance (a fixed point) between the telling of the story and the events of the story?

Why? (Theme). Why does this story *have* to be told? Why is it important to the characters and/or the narrator? What's at stake emotionally, intellectually, or morally? What haunts this story?

How? (Craft/Art/Narrative Strategy). How does the story operate? How is it designed? How does it make its meaning? Below are more specific questions of craft that get at this crucial "how" question.

Point of View? What is the point of view of the story? First person (present tense, retrospective, reliable, unreliable, plural)? Second person? Third person (effaced, limited omniscience, rotating limited omniscience, neutral or chatty omniscience)? How does this point of view serve the story? Why does the story have to be told from this perspective?

Mode/Form? Does the story employ a particular mode or form of storytelling? Psychological realism? Parable, fable, allegory? Surrealism? Magical realism? Is the story a tragedy, a comedy, a satire, a romance? Is it a coming-of-age story (*bildungsroman, künstlerroman*)? Does it combine or blur genres in an interesting way?

Structure/Shape/Design? Is there a discernable shape, structure, or narrative design? Is the story episodic? Does it lead to an emotional or intellectual epiphany? Is there a journey or mock journey? Can you identify the parts of the story (exposition, rising action, climax, falling action, and denouement)? Does the narrative have a linear or mosaic design? How does that design encode or unleash the energy of the story?

Tone? What is the author's attitude toward the story and/or the characters? Earnest, ironic, satiric, tragic, comic, absurdist? What attitude does the author ask the reader to take toward the characters and story?

Style/Language? Is the style accessible, plain-spoken, direct, minimalist, intellectual, removed? Is it ornate, dense, lyrical, metaphorical, emotional? How does the style reflect the deepest purpose or meaning of the story? How does it affect *your* reading of the story? Does the style intentionally or unintentionally facilitate or inhibit your understanding of the narrative and access to the inner lives of the characters?

Imagery/Patterning? Do words or images in the story accumulate meaning or create echoes? Do any words or images rise to the level of symbol? Do these accumulated images and words suggest a way of understanding the story? Are there actions that repeat? If so, what is the significance of this rhyming action?

A Text-Centered Response

Below is an example of a workshop response to Carver's "Popular Mechanics" that uses these questions as prompts in a more descriptive, analytical, text-centered critique.

> Hey Big Ray—
>
> *What (Plot) & Who (Characters).* A man, a woman, and their baby. They've obviously just had a major argument. The story thrusts us into the aftermath. He angrily packs his things. He's done something bad. Had an affair? Struck her? Gambled away their savings? We're not sure, but whatever he's done, she believes him to be a "son of a bitch," and she's "so glad" he's leaving. Yet she feels deeply ambivalent; her taunts are quickly followed by tears. Maybe it was she who did whatever is prompting his departure; maybe she's using his departure to rationalize her behavior. As she cries, she tells him, "You can't even look at me in the face." She wants evidence of his remorse,

his shame. Or is she saying this because she feels guilty about what she did? Both seem to be at fault, and their mutual complicity intensifies as the story progresses. She sees the picture of the baby on the bed, picks it up, and leaves the room. This engages him—perhaps that's her intention—and he demands she return the picture and then demands that she also give him the baby, not because he wants the child but rather because the baby is the very thing that he knows she will not give up. Their argument escalates into a physical struggle—the only way now for this couple to come together—with them knocking over a flowerpot and him pinning her against the wall, where he "worked on her fisted fingers with one hand and with the other hand gripped the screaming baby up under an arm near the shoulder." They both "would have it, this baby," and neither will let go until the baby is seemingly pulled apart.

Where (Setting) & When (Time). The setting is anywhere contemporary America. The couple lives in a small house or, more likely, an apartment. We can sense the claustrophobia, the cramped quarters—a toppled flowerpot, walls that the woman can be pinned against, only one or two bedrooms. It's a winter's day, near dusk. The snow falls, turning into "dirty water." The light fades. Ominously, "it was getting dark on the inside too." The scene takes place in real time, perhaps only a few minutes, but as the struggle becomes more violent, the darkness inside this home asserts its symbolic presence: "The kitchen gave no light" as he "worked on her fisted fingers" in "the near dark."

Why (Theme). In a climax reminiscent of Solomon and the two mothers arguing over possession of an infant, the parents each grab the baby and literally rend the child in two. "In this manner," the narrator says in the chillingly ironic final line, "the issue was decided." The story suggests that this kind of marital conflict is all too common, all too "popular," and that everyone in the family suffers—especially the innocent child. The story refuses, however, to let us feel much empathy or sympathy for either the husband or the wife. The argument is de-contextualized; we don't know what it's about and, the story implies, it doesn't really matter. Nothing can justify what happens here. We are given little to no entry into the consciousness of either character, certainly no sympathetic access. And the story cuts away after the characters have perpetrated their crime. We know the baby is injured or perhaps dead, but we are not allowed to see the grief or remorse of the parents. We simply know—in the passive voice of the judicial process—that this is "the manner" in which the issue "was decided."

Point of View. For the most part, the point of view is neutral, effaced, simply describing the action of the characters as if a camera has captured the scene. At times, the effaced description gives way to a tight-lipped omniscience, as in the symbolic line at the end of the first paragraph: "But it was getting dark on the inside too." As the story closes, the narrative voice subtly enters the consciousness of the wife as she "felt her fingers being forced open" and "felt the baby going from her." But we are not allowed to feel much empathy for her because these lines are quickly followed by a flash of insight into her will and intention: "She would have it, this baby." The baby, like the picture earlier, is merely an object to fight over, a way to stay emotionally fused to her husband. The only entry into the man's perspective occurs at the end with this line: "He felt the baby slipping out of his hands." After the final action, the narrative voice abruptly shifts from the aftermath of the tragedy and pronounces, with devastating understatement, that in "this manner, the issue was decided."

Mode/Form/Shape. The story has the pared-down quality not so much of modernist or contemporary minimalism but rather of ancient parable. In a parable, the narrative, characters, and style are all skeletal. A father with two sons, for instance—one faithful, one prodigal. A husband, a wife, a baby. The narrative reinforces a moral lesson: look who suffers the most in this conflict of wills? The biblical story this piece echoes, as I mentioned, is Solomon and the two mothers. In both narratives a baby is—or is threatened to be—torn in two by competing parents. Yet, in the vision of this story, no true parent relents in order to save the baby. No wise Solomon decides the issue.

Tone & Style. The style is spare, common for parables, forgoing the kind of rigorous detail (character names, exposition) and conventions of punctuation (quotation marks) that would ground it more firmly in psychological realism. The title alludes to the wide-circulation blue-collar magazine, *Popular Mechanics,* but also serves as a pronouncement on not just this couple but a culture in which these kind of family "mechanics" are all too common. The final line not only has biblical overtones, both in its diction and formality, but is also shocking in its tonal shift. We see this struggle in close-up (those fisted fingers being worked on). Then the narrative abruptly stops at the most violent moment. That blackout, with its passive-voice judicial understatement, is both a chilling indictment and a form of linguistic violence.

Imagery/Patterning. There seem to be two dominant image patterns. The first: the imagery of light and dark. The fading light in this house suggests a physical, psychological, and moral darkness overtaking the home and alerts us to the traditional biblical form, allusions, and symbolism of the story. The second pattern of imagery involves the language of "wresting"—of both "mechanics" and of violent struggle. These characters are "pushing," "holding," "hurting." They "scuffle" and "knock down." Their hands are "fisted" and "worked on," "gripped" and "forced open." They grab and pull. As the darkness envelops this couple, they find that what they most want, what they most care about, is "slipping" from them.

Way to go, Big Ray. You *do* rock, man! See you at Lyzzard's at 4:15. I'll bring my own pool cue, thank you very much.

—Kenneth

P.S. I disagree with Kenardo's suggestion in workshop about changing the title. "Popular Mechanics" reinforces the dark irony of this story (and by the way, I think you're good at irony), and it forces the reader back into the story. "Little Things" simplifies the meaning, which may be in keeping with the parable form, but it also potentially sentimentalizes what happens to this family.

What I like most about this text-centered approach is that it focuses squarely on the story itself. It does not make assumptions about the circumstances of the writing or the writer. Most importantly, it forces the responder to read carefully, to describe and interpret what happens on the page rather than providing half-baked, unsubstantiated indictments or praise. This method values the rigorous text-based strategies for critiquing that the New Critics of the mid-twentieth century espoused—literary criticism that privileges close formal examination—a necessary pragmatic approach for writers, rooted in attention to craft.

Perhaps surprisingly, this kind of critique is not only more thorough, but more generous. The responder honors the text and the writer by treating it seriously as a work of art. The responder, rather than offering a critique, seeks to understand the piece, to fully digest, distill, describe, and appreciate it, and to figure out *how* it works in terms of form and technique. This strategy has the added benefit of putting the onus of responsibility on the one offering the critique rather than the writer being workshopped. The responder, in effect, must prove worthy of offering suggestions or advice, based on the depth and persuasiveness of the description and analysis. If the responder has misread the story, then the writer can either discount the criticism or re-evaluate his or her intentions, especially if the misreading is more persuasive and interesting than the story itself, which frequently and productively happens in the best workshops.

Such an extended response is useful, not only for the writer, but for the responder and for the group as a whole. This level of preparation inevitably enriches the experience of the workshop itself. If one of the main goals of workshop is to help writers learn how to read more carefully in order to develop their craft and aesthetic judgment, then a consistently rigorous practice of response is crucial to that development.

What's problematic about this kind of descriptive critique? There is a tendency toward repetition because there will always be overlap between the various elements of fiction that I've parsed out for the purpose of analysis. It's also not as personal and, in fact, can seem a little too formal, even aloof, which does not always address the inherent vulnerability of writers. The appreciation of the story is perhaps too implicit; it doesn't convey, except indirectly, what the responder admired or found compelling, distinctive, or bold about the piece. Most importantly, it leaves out questions, issues, or suggestions.

Except for the postscript, it doesn't investigate, through critical *evaluation* (as opposed to critical *appreciation*), what may be at cross-purposes within the work, where it fails to engage, or where it is just plain confusing.

Describe/Praise/Question Response

In my workshops, we spend at least half the time doing this descriptive, analytical, and interpretive work. I often assign an individual to begin with the kind of formal analysis above, and then the rest of us clarify, modify, unpack, and add to the initial responder's critique. We spend significant time, in other words, treating the work as a piece of literature.

Then we turn our attention to what is most compelling about the piece, what most moves, provokes, disturbs, or fascinates us, what is bold and risky, and even what we unabashedly love. Praise and aesthetic pleasure are crucial to the workshop process. Writers need genuine encouragement and clarity about where and how they have succeeded in order to do the hard work of re-envisioning the text. Finally, we move toward a questions/issues/suggestions phase that is framed around questions and concerns rather than prescriptive fixes—the goal being to get the writer and the entire group to think, in an open-ended way, about specific issues of clarity, form, technique, aesthetics, ambition, and taste. I want us to consider the alternate possibilities inherent, but perhaps unrealized, in the work.

Here is what this kind of describe/praise/question model of response might look like for Big Ray's "Popular Mechanics":

Dear Big Ray—

Description/Interpretation

This story is a tragic parable. An unnamed man and woman argue. As the man packs his bags and prepares to leave, presumably because of something one of them has done to damage the relationship, his wife tearfully berates him for his or her (unspecified) bad behavior and says she's glad he's leaving. He tells her that he wants their baby, and when she refuses, their argument turns physical—and ultimately violent—as the husband and wife both refuse to give up the child.

In a climax eerily reminiscent of Solomon and the two mothers fighting over possession of a child, the parents each grab the baby and seem to literally rend the child in two. "In this manner," the narrator says in the ironic final line, "the issue was decided." The story suggests that this kind of marital conflict is all too common, all too "popular," and that everyone in the family suffers—especially the innocent child.

Praise

This story scared me—as it moves from what seems like a typical argument between a husband and wife to an event that takes on biblical proportions. Normally, I do not like stories that lack specificity and that seem this generalized. (No names, no specific place.) But the pared-down quality of the story haunted me and made me think of it as a dark parable. Your ending forced me to imagine what happened after "the issue was decided," and what I imagined was more horrific than what you might have described. The final line—which sounded judicial and formal, with its passive voice—haunted me for a long time after I read the story.

I admired your "staging" of the event. It reads like a play with very little access to the inner lives of the characters. Everything we learn about them is based on their dialogue and actions. Although I had some reservations about your point of view (see below), the story is dramatically told; the scuffle over the baby builds momentum until the shattering climax.

Questions/Issues/Suggestions

Inconsistent POV? Is the somewhat inconsistent point of view of this story problematic—the way it shifts at the end from an effaced point of view to a tight-lipped, though somewhat judgmental, omniscience? Maybe stay out of their heads completely to avoid the inconsistency.

Whose Bad Behavior? Right now, it's not clear whose bad behavior has triggered the man's departure. The woman castigates the man, so my sense is that he is at fault, but we never learn for sure. Do we need to know? Or is the ambiguity about who might be to blame for the breakup consistent with the end of the story, where both are culpable in what happens to the baby?

Final Line? Is that final sentence, with its judicial tone and biblical allusions and ironies, too jarring? Is it "earned," as Kenardo would say? Or is the shock of that final line actually an indication of the story's ambition, its willingness to be morally tough with the characters' transgressions? I feel ambivalent about my response.

Parable Form? Does this story effectively communicate the cross-genre mixture of parable and psychological realism? What is the effect of that genre mixing? Does the parable form, with its sometimes heavy-handed symbolism, seem too reductive or old-fashioned for a contemporary reader, who (like me) typically craves greater particularity and complexity, with less overt authorial judgment?

Minimalism? Is the story too pared down, too minimalistic? What would be gained or lost by loosening the tight reins of the story and allowing the reader greater and more immediate access to the consciousness of one or more of the characters?

Repetition? What purpose does the repetition (he said, she said, baby, etc.) serve?

Punctuation? What do you gain by eliminating the quotation marks from the story?

Title? What about that title? Is it too oblique, too ironic? Would an alternative title, something like "Little Things," sentimentalize the story too much?

A haunting piece of sudden fiction, Big Ray. Good luck with your revision.

—Kenny

Such a response attempts first to understand the story, then praises it specifically, before it critically evaluates it. When I offer my critique or suggestions, I try not to do so in a prescriptive way but rather in a more open-ended, investigative way that invites "Big Ray" back into the story. Big Ray, of course, is not required to take any of this advice. In fact, the description and the praise may—and often are—the most valuable elements for the writer in this kind of workshop. Questions have the power to open up the imagination in a way that suggestions don't.

Workshop as Gift Community

The writer is not, I would argue, the primary beneficiary of workshop. The other participants are the main beneficiaries. The work before us is, I frequently remind my students, a gift for our aesthetic laboratory. We get to play with the possibilities of a text without feeling enmeshed in the messy, multi-draft, emotionally fraught process of creation. Workshop should help everybody understand the opportunities of re-visioning. Those possibilities are frequently easier to recognize and contemplate in the drafts of peers rather than one's own work.

The ultimate objective, in this model of workshop, is to shift the qualitative balance of discussion and encourage students, both in their written critiques and in the workshop setting itself, to devote half (if not more) of the time to description, analysis, and interpretation, exploring the assumptions and meanings embedded in a text. This process presumes that the work contains a certain level of professional and artistic intentionality.

Such an approach, I've found, deepens and broadens the level of discourse. It also has the extraordinary benefit of treating students as serious artists, whose work demands not only respect but rigorous interpretive attention, both critical appreciation *and* critical evaluation. Even if the student's work does not yet merit this kind of scrutiny, the very process honors the potential of that writer to eventually produce work that will, in the future, be worthy of such focused care. Workshop teachers shouldn't expect to transform their students into the next Shakespeares, Austens, Faulkners, or Morrisons. Brilliance can't necessarily be taught. Talent in young artists, though, can and must be nurtured and refined, and extensive practice with pragmatic, text-centered criticism is a crucial part of that refinement.

The main goal of the workshop leader, I believe, is to design a process that encourages students to become more alert, passionate, precise, constructive, and creative readers and critics. Teachers and practitioners in other arts—music, fine arts, dance, theatre, film—understand this obvious goal. Our job is not necessarily to improve the stories of our students, but rather to foster a genuine love of the art as well as increasingly sophisticated ways of comprehending, discussing, and practicing it. For a teacher, that is the crucial and, I would argue, the most honorable ambition.

We often think, when we agree to be part of a workshop, that what we most desire is to have the flaws of our stories, poems, essays, and scripts pointed out to us so that we can correct them, to be in a group that will help us hone our skills so that we can be more self-sufficient in discovering the problems in our work ourselves. That's an important part of it, certainly. But what we really want, at the deepest level, is to have our stories, novels, poems, essays, and scripts *understood* and *appreciated*. And we want to learn how to better understand and appreciate others' works, to extend our aesthetic comprehension, range, and taste, and to evaluate based on our ability first to articulate our comprehension and appreciation. The workshop process, at its best, illuminates what the writer may only inchoately recognize about the piece. Description, analysis, interpretation, and inquiry teach us what is already there in the work but may not yet be visible to us.

Workshop should be a haven of generosity—a place where we, first and foremost, respect both the work and the complex vulnerability of the writer, and so strive to meet the work on its own terms, to genuinely appreciate it before we critique it. What I have imported from my training in literature (and in theatre)—as well as from my occasional bad experiences in workshop—is the assumption that the work is *worthy* of our attention, that it is, however misshapen, an attempt at literature. Such an assumption will carry the writer through the difficulties of revision; it will, more times than not, invite the writer back into the work to discover its mysteries and essential energy. Regardless, such an assumption and approach make for a livelier, more interesting, and more rigorously focused conversation, useful for everyone, not just the writer being workshopped.

Ideally, the workshop should reinforce the spirit of gift communities. In his groundbreaking work on the condition of the artist in the modern world, *The Gift*, Lewis Hyde describes and explores the psychological, spiritual, and erotic dimensions of gift communities, gift cultures, and gifts of the imagination. This passage from Hyde suggests, to my mind, the secret power of workshops at their best:

> When a gift passes from hand to hand in this spirit, it becomes the binder of many wills. What gathers in it is not only the sentiment of generosity but the affirmation of individual goodwill, making of those separate parts a *spiritus mundi,* a unanimous heart, a band whose wills are focused through the lens of the gift. Thus the gift becomes an agent of social cohesion, and this again leads to the feeling that its passage increases its worth, for in social life, at least, the whole really is greater than the sum of its parts. If it brings the group together, the gift increases in worth immediately upon its first circulation, and then, like a faithful lover, continues to grow through constancy.

Workshop is most consistently relevant, is most persuasive and galvanizing, when the level of discourse first honors the offerings of each participant as if those offerings were gifts. When we receive a gift, we do not immediately critique it. We describe and praise it, to let the giver know that we understand its subtleties and appreciate its virtues and the spirit with which it was given.

When the workshop disintegrates into a method of fault-finding in which the participants pride themselves on their attention to technique, to the exclusion of other considerations, or into merely a subjective expression of each reader's tastes, biases, predilections, and moods, then it violates the essential spirit of gift-giving. Cultivating the spirit of gift exchange in one's critique benefits not just the writer whose work is being discussed but all involved.

And the benefits transcend craft. A gift culture enlivens the spirit and reinforces a belief in the inherent value of creation as an affirming and necessary process. No matter what methodology we use in our workshops, our first priority should be to articulate, create, and nurture this kind of generous exchange and community.

Forms of Fiction

The Pleasures of Form

In *Narrative Design,* Madison Smartt Bell suggests that "we are all continually in the process of learning to apprehend narrative structures, in their integrity and in their best possible wholeness.... The reader who wants to write as well has got to go beyond the intuitive grasp of form to the deliberate construction of form."

Form is, I believe, the most difficult element of craft for any writer, especially the fiction writer, to understand and master. It can, and probably *should,* take a lifetime. That's certainly been the case for me. In all of my stories and books, both the published and unpublished ones, I strive to understand not only my subject but also how to give my narratives the most effective shape and focus. That has sometimes been a painfully long process, but in most cases, it's been a source of aesthetic pleasure and an integral part of my apprenticeship and ongoing development as a writer. Helping my students figure out their subject matter and discover the traditions and forms that give their stories meaning has been and continues to be one of my more important goals as teacher. Form, in fact, is the element of craft that most affects the design and organization of my creative writing courses—courses such as Sudden Fiction, Short Story Cycle, and Forms of Fiction. The primary thing I've learned is that there is no magic recipe, no special secret. There are, instead, many different ways to think about form. I'd like to briefly discuss five of those ways.

Length. Length, of course, is the primary determinant of form in fiction, dictating practical issues about plotting, pacing, and characterization, as well as basic assumptions about what exactly a story *is*. For instance, if you're writing sudden fiction (also known as short-shorts and flash fiction), you're dealing with methods of narrative compression and traditions that depend on brevity (e.g., jokes, parables, and fables, among others). Sudden fiction exists in a liminal space, with as much kinship to poetry as fiction. As a narrative lengthens, the demands, expectations, and pleasures change. When considering form in terms of length, we focus on the differences between narrative summary, half-scene, and scene. The shorter the narrative, the more reliant it will be on summary (on *telling*); the longer the narrative, the more reliant it will be on scene (*showing*). That old workshop cliché—"show don't tell"—is a relative truth, depending entirely upon the length and scope of the narrative.

Shape, Structure, Design. Beyond length, what we often mean by form is shape, structure, and design. Plot, in other words, and the relationship between structure and meaning. We can, for instance, think of Homer's *The*

Odyssey as having the *shape* of a journey. Its plot, however, is *structured* around the twelve different stops of that journey—a structure that James Joyce famously mimicked and deconstructed in his mock-epic, *Ulysses*. Those who conceive of form in terms of shape, structure, and design are essentially Aristotelians, concerned primarily with the artful and suspenseful presentation and arrangement (and at times subversion) of exposition, rising action, climax, falling action, and denouement.

Genre. We can also think about form in terms of genre. Unfortunately, there's not been much serious teaching of genre, at least not in most college and university workshop settings. Genre has a bad reputation, carrying with it the taint of commercialism. When asked by people, "What kind of writing do you do?" I usually answer, "Literary fiction," which is considered a genre category by publishers. When asked what that means, my stock response is: "Writing that doesn't make any money." Despite my flippancy, I do believe that genre is an important method of conceptualizing form in fiction. Genre is, in fact, the way most writers over the millennia have thought about form. Most of our best writers are actually great students and critics of genre—not just Sophocles, Shakespeare, Cervantes, Austen, the Bronte sisters, and Twain, but also Marquez, Doctorow, Proulx, Updike, Rushdie, Oates,

Morrison, Roth, McCarthy, DeLillo, Gordimer, and Lessing.

"Though the fact is not always obvious at a glance," John Gardner says in *The Art of Fiction,* "the artist's primary unit of thought—his primary conscious or unconscious basis for selecting and organizing the details of his work—is genre." Although I'm intrigued by the many categories and subcategories of popular genres, I prefer the classical genre archetypes—romance, comedy, tragedy, and satire—which are still valuable in conveying to readers, through form, the meaning of a text. Romance, the genre of love and passion, for instance, emphasizes the beautiful and orderly, and presents an idealized vision of the world. Comedy, the genre of inclusivity and revelry, begins with characters in a state of opposition to one another and moves, through conflict, toward individual and communal harmony. Tragedy is the genre most concerned with irrevocable error and the process of death and disintegration—the end of things, the elegiac spirit, the aesthetics of suffering. Satire is the genre of anger, of criticism and social correction, using ridicule and exaggeration to expose hypocrisy and injustice. Writers should explore the emotional purpose and social function of these archetypal genres and the way these forms allow us to communicate with our readers.

Technique. Technique is another essential way to think about form. There are hundreds of specific literary techniques, certainly too many for any one writer to contemplate, much less master—especially if technique is considered simply a grab-bag of tricks or tools for your toolbox. Instead, I find it more useful to think about literary technique in the context of larger aesthetic movements: classic, modernist, and postmodernist. Classic fictive techniques, for instance, focus on strategies for achieving unity of action in service of a high moral purpose. These strategies are often governed by assumptions about the moral value and authority of storytelling, beautiful symmetry, and complete rather than provisional resolution. Classic writers essentially believe in the two ancient goals of literature: entertainment and instruction. Fiction is primarily a tool for exploring values, morality, and ethics.

In the first half of the twentieth century, modernist writers were less interested in moral instruction and more concerned with accurately depicting consciousness. They developed techniques of narration that subtly examined the unconscious life. Influenced by the breakthroughs of Freud and Einstein, among other intellectuals, the modernists also subverted traditional conceptions of authority, truth, and objectivity. Most of the formal strategies and techniques that evolved from the modernist movement concentrate on new ways of fracturing time and handling point of view.

The postmodernist movement that began in the second half of the twentieth century intensified the modernist impulse to deconstruct traditional forms of storytelling and examine not only consciousness but self-consciousness. If you're a postmodernist, then you are perhaps the most form-obsessed writer, because the motive behind postmodernism is to reveal storytelling as an artificial, self-referential process. To tear something apart means that you have to know how (and why) it was constructed in the first place. Postmodernist techniques aim to deconstruct and reshape classic and modernist notions of storytelling, exposing the suspect processes of creation and the slippery nature of any kind of narrative truth.

Fortunately, we're all post-postmodernists now. That means we don't have to be faithful to any of these philosophical assumptions or technical approaches to form. We have access to all of them. A quick glance at the Pulitzer Prize winners in fiction over the last two decades reveals just how eclectic our literary tastes have become—with classic writers such as Richard Russo standing alongside modernists like Michael Cunningham and postmodernists like Jennifer Egan.

Post-Postmodernist Discourses. Jane Smiley, also a Pulitzer Prize winner, presents a compelling way, in *13 Ways of Looking at the Novel,* for the post-postmodernist writer to think about fictional form. She especially encourages writers to examine fiction in relation to earlier forms of narrative discourse—but not necessarily with the goal of deconstruction or subversion. The difficulty for the novelist, she says, is that she or he "always has to contend with the fact that the novel is an essentially compromised form.... It grew out of earlier types of literature and can't be understood except by reference to them."

The easiest way to conceptualize the novel, she suggests, is to "imagine an analog clock face with the novel in the middle and the forms of discourse it's related to arranged around the circumference." The clock has twelve stations: Travel Narrative, History, Biography, Tale, Joke, Gossip, Diary/Letters, Confession, Polemic, Essay, Epic, and Romance. "Each station represents a specific type of discourse. Each type has essential characteristics and offers the reader a particular form of pleasure." Form for the fiction writer then is a matter of figuring out how and to what degree the story or novel you're working on taps into the energy of these different modes of discourse. Excellence and innovation arise from a deep awareness and clever recombination of these various discourses—a conscious and energetic mash-up. This is, I believe, a particularly liberating way of conceiving the art and craft of fiction writing.

"Form is primary," Madison Smart Bell suggests, "whatever defines it. In the beginning, through the middle and all the way to the end, form is what orients both writer and reader within a text. All other elements are melodic, not structural. You must learn to play melodies too. But the form of a work is its skeleton, if not its heart." I know, as a writer and as a longtime student and teacher of fiction, that form is the one thing I can continue learning and teaching for the rest of my life—the one thing that will remain a source of endless aesthetic pleasure and mystery.

Every Story Is a Love Song

A few years ago, frustrated with the long novel I'd been laboring over, I turned (or rather returned) to short stories—my first love. I found it refreshing and liberating to move from story to story, to actually *finish* pieces and send them to editors and have them published. My work with these stories also led to experimentation with other short forms—sudden fiction, poems, lyric essays, memoir, personal essays, and criticism.

At a certain point, I realized that I had more than enough stories for a book—about thirty-five pieces, some as long as twelve thousand words, some as short as two hundred. But I wanted the book to be a thematically organized short story cycle, with its own integrity and unity, not a conventional collection of miscellaneous tales. I wanted the stories to talk to, counterpoint, inform, and build upon one another, creating a cumulative aesthetic effect. I wanted the whole to be greater than the sum of its parts, which is my guiding principle when selecting and organizing a collection of stories.

The process of tracking the patterns and discovering the secret design in my own work revealed to me both conscious and unconscious obsessions. It reminded me that putting together a collection of stories is a vital act of not just revision but investigation and *re-visioning*. And that, I believe, is what we're all after, as writers—to discover what haunts and inspires us and to find more conscious ways of getting that on the page.

One of my stories was about an epidemic of whooping cough that quarantines a family of four. I was surprised to discover that many of the characters in my other pieces seemed quarantined in one way or another—not just physically, but also emotionally, psychologically, erotically, spiritually. There were hospitals and diseases and recoveries, of course, but also figurative forms of isolation—especially as the characters contemplated their destinies and obligations to families, friends, and lovers. My first attempt at organization resulted in a rather heavy-handed symbolic structure. The book, in this incarnation, contained twenty-five stories, was called *Quarantine,* and was divided into five sections that reflected a sickness-to-healing progression: Exposure, Intensive Care, Quarantine, Experimental Treatment, and Miraculous Recovery.

I saw the book coming together as a unified collection, but I was nonetheless dissatisfied with the overall thematic design. It seemed too dark in tone, masking what was comic, playful, and redemptive in the stories. These pieces weren't relentlessly grim. Many were celebratory, even ecstatic, in spirit. My agent once said to me, "Every story is a love story," which made me think of two of my favorite stories, touchstones that I return to again and again for inspiration—Anton Chekhov's "The Lady with the Pet Dog" and James Baldwin's "Sonny's Blues." Both are love stories, both love songs. Without knowing it, I had been writing with that idea in mind and perhaps with these two stories as my litmus tests for what a story should be, what complexity of emotion it can or should embody. My stories were, in fact, love songs—to spouses and lovers, to children, to parents, to siblings, to friends, to mentors.

Clearly I had been fascinated, in ways I didn't realize consciously, by the unexpected transformations in our lives, how we embrace or resist isolation and solitude, how we become quarantined—or, more often, quarantine ourselves. But it now seemed equally obvious that I was also obsessed with the ways we respond to suffering—the ways we console one another and ourselves in times of grief, the ways we find not just solace but pleasure. That's what love songs are all about—joy and resiliency in the face of suffering. With this in mind, I now worked to wed these two thematic strands—quarantine and love songs.

I kept thinking about the haunting beginning of T. S. Eliot's "The Love Song of J. Alfred Prufrock":

> Let us go then, you and I,
> When the evening is spread out against the sky,
> Like a patient etherized upon a table....

I wanted, like Eliot, through Prufrock, to take readers on an intimate journey. I wanted to take their hands and head out under that ominous sky. I wanted to share these stories, these songs, about a visit from Bonnie and Clyde, about brothers hearing disturbing prophecies from a fortune teller, about a comic snipe hunt taking on terrifying resonance, about two siblings coping with another's suicide, about a couple's precarious journey into full-throttle parenthood.

Once I figured out this essential intention—this core of yearning—in my work, I was able to reorganize the stories, cutting those that didn't serve the larger thematic and narrative design and revising with the idea that every one of the final sixteen stories was a song. A love song for the quarantined.

Which became, in the end, the title of the book.

The Secret Story: Rituals of Revelation

About a decade ago, I was teaching an MFA novel workshop. My own credentials at the time came from publishing a couple of books—*Last Call,* a thirty-year family saga in the form of linked stories, and *The Girl from Charnelle,* a more traditionally structured novel about a sixteen-year-old girl grappling with the disappearance of her mother, as well as her own affair with a married man. As a way of talking about the form and tradition of the novel, I assigned Tim O'Brien's *In the Lake of the Woods,* an award-winning literary novel about a politician who hides his participation in the notorious Mai Lai incident during the Vietnam War, only to be publicly humiliated during the election when the secret is revealed and he is not only trounced in the polls but must rectify his relationship with his wife.

Among the eclectic group of workshop manuscripts, there was a paranormal post-apocalyptic Western, a road trip story involving a desperate makeshift family on the run, a *roman à clef* about a girl raised in an incestuous home with her tyrannical fundamentalist preacher father, and two young adult novels, one a fantasy epic and the other a Dickensian-inspired tale in which a young orphan discovers his true identity.

Although I didn't realize it during my preparation, it became clear in discussion that each book we workshopped, as well as others we referenced, dealt in an essential way with secrets. The protagonists of all these books—including Tim O'Brien's and my own—were urgently engaged in some level of secrecy maintenance. They were keeping secrets from others, and the plots revolved around the stratagems of deceit and the danger of revelation. Or the protagonists actively investigated the crimes and mysteries of other people, other relationships, or entire cultural, social, or spiritual systems. Or the goal of the plot—as with the paranormal post-apocalyptic Western and the fantasy epic—was to reveal a meta-secret about the origins or workings of an alternative universe. We were all surprised by this coincidence.

"Maybe all stories are really about secrets and revelations," I said, and we pondered that possibility throughout the week of discussions.

Afterwards, I began doing more intensive research on the subject. I analyzed my own work more carefully in light of this epiphany. I reflected on my family's history, which inspired much of my fiction. I grew up in a home where many secrets were kept. My father was a pyramid-scheme salesman and later a con-man who died in Las Vegas, trying to make his fortune. His brother went to prison for international mail fraud, and my father lived his short life in fear that he might be heading there as well. My mother married twelve times, and often one husband was moving out as another was moving in. I grew up only half-understanding what my parents were involved in. When I was drawn into their secrets, I often felt forced, against my will, to be a confidant and accomplice, trained in the suppression, maintenance, or elaboration of secrets.

I also began to examine more carefully the fiction I was reading. I was a judge for two national fiction contests during this time, so I had the opportunity to evaluate a large volume of recently published contemporary novels and collections of stories. And I continued to read, in my role as a creative writing and literature professor, thousands of pages each year of undergraduate and graduate fiction, while I was also teaching a wide range of literature courses—including a Shakespeare seminar, a Family Systems in Film and Literature course, and the Literature of the American Dream.

Rituals of Revelation

I now believe all narratives, all plots, all stories are really about the suppression or revelation of secrets, as well as the consequences of that suppression or revelation. A plot is, literally, a secret plan. Mystery implies a hidden realm waiting to be discovered. An epiphany reveals an unknown truth—a "showing forth," as James Joyce said. On one level, this all seems quite obvious. *A story of secrets and lies* is the tag line of many novels, films, and television shows. But what I'm suggesting is that secrecy is not just the subject or theme of most, if not all, stories. It is the defining structural feature—its *form*. Every plot, at its core, is a ritual of revelation.

What does this ritual look like? A secret is established and, under great strain, maintained until it is finally revealed through confession or exposure. Reckonings ensue, culminating in physical, emotional, psychological, legal, and/or spiritual recalibrations for the characters and, by extension, the reader or audience. The ritual follows this progression:

Secret → Revelation → Reckoning → Recalibration

Many plots scramble the linearity of this progression, and writers place weight on different elements of the ritual. *The Great Gatsby,* for instance, begins in a state of emotional and moral recalibration for Nick Carraway, as he ponders the aftermath of Gatsby's death. Most Faulkner plots are nonlinear puzzles full of nested secrets. Toni Morrison revisits again and again the circumstances of Sethe's murder of her daughter in *Beloved,* though the novel's emotional core is the long-term emotional reckoning and moral recalibration following her desperate act.

Regardless of the sequencing, these four elements—secrecy, revelation, reckoning, and recalibration—are essential to every plot.

Types of Secrecy Plots

Although there are infinite permutations on this ritual of revelation, there are three primary types of secrecy plots.

Secret-Keeping. Plots in which characters attempt to keep secrets from others. Think of Richard III, Macbeth, Iago, the disguised heroines in most of Shakespeare's comedies, Raskolnikov in *Crime and Punishment,* Don Draper in *Mad Men,* Walter White in *Breaking Bad,* Elizabeth and Philip in *The Americans*. In secret-keeping plots, the author makes the reader/audience complicit in the protagonist's secret—a sin, a crime, a transgression, or a matter of self-protection. We know, at least intuitively, from the logic of plot, that the protagonist must eventually confess or get caught, and the suspense in these kinds of narratives pivots on whether the confession or the unmasking will happen first, and what the consequences of the revelation will be. As readers and audience members, we feel the conflicting desire for continued suppression and exposure of the secret.

Investigations. Plots in which characters actively investigate secrets. Think of Oedipus in search of the killer of the previous king (not knowing that he in fact is the criminal who must be punished), or Hamlet feigning madness and concocting a "mousetrap" in order to verify the guilt of his uncle-king, or Sherlock Holmes or any Agatha Christie detective or *CSI* investigator. The primary pleasure we take in these plots is the pleasure of solving a riddle or bringing a criminal to justice. Sometimes, however, the "investigator" is passive or an unwilling recipient of a revelation that endangers him or her—as in Joyce Carol Oates' iconic story, "Where Are You Going, Where Have You Been?" in which Connie, the adolescent protagonist, suddenly realizes that Arnold Friend, the boy who has driven out to her house on a Sunday afternoon to presumably flirt with her, is in actuality a thirty-year-old satanic figure who has come to do her and her family harm.

Macro-Secrets. Plots involving a macro-secret about the origins of the narrative world. Think of the plots of many works of sci-fi, fantasy, dystopian, or speculative fiction, in which the macro-narrative involves the revelation that, for example, the Planet of the Apes is really Earth or the ingredients of Soylent Green are humans. Or, to use a higher-quality example, think of the brilliant slow reveal of the circumstances that led to the patriarchal theocracy of Gilead in Margaret Atwood's *The Handmaid's Tale*. Atwood keeps the narrative tightly focused on the handmaid Offred and her attempt to make sense of, negotiate, and escape from this nightmare, but the larger secrets that the reader yearns to know are how things got to be this way and how the seeds of this dystopian world are embedded in our own culture.

Scope and Ubiquity

The more compressed the narrative, the less pressure there is to dramatize all four stages of a secrecy plot. In a lyric poem, a piece of flash fiction, or a short story, the whole text may consist simply of, for example, the revelation scene—the character apprehending a mystery in a luminous moment of paralysis. The emotional, psychological, or spiritual recalibrations are implied by the graceful articulation of the revelation. James Joyce's "Araby" famously ends with an epiphanic moment of self-awareness, characteristic of the conclusions of most of his stories: "Gazing up in the darkness I saw myself as a creature driven and derided by vanity; and my eyes burned with anguish and anger." The epiphany is both a revelation and a key moment of reckoning—a boy recognizing and condemning his own vanity and foolishness.

The longer the narrative, the more necessary it is for the writer to deliver on all four stages of a secrecy plot. In fact, the longer the narrative, the more the writer may need multiple fully formed and interwoven secrecy plots, as we see in practically every Shakespearean play. Iago masterfully hides his false identity from Othello and all the other characters, while simultaneously setting in motion an investigatory plot in which he and Othello search for evidence (what the Moor calls "the ocular proof") of Desdemona's infidelity. Hamlet may be investigating the murder of his father, but all the other characters are investigating the source of Hamlet's own erratic behavior. In *Les Misérables,* Hugo counterpoints Jean Valjean's secret-keeping plot with, among other subplots, Inspector Javert's attempts to investigate Valjean's identity and bring him to justice. The novel's (and stage and screen adaptations') highest moments of tension and power involve the revelation and reckoning scenes that pit Valjean and Javert against one another and force the two to recalibrate their actions as a result of their confessions and discoveries.

Secrecy plots are also ubiquitous in series television. Walter White, the mild-mannered high school science teacher turned meth kingpin in *Breaking Bad,* spends five seasons frantically keeping his identity a secret, while his brother-in-law, a DEA agent, slowly closes in on the criminal in his own family. Each season is punctuated by crucial revelations of that secret identity to characters close to Walter, and new episodes and seasons unspool from the reckonings and recalibrations that result from those revelations. One of the addictive pleasures of the British television series *Downton Abbey* is the way the creator Julian Fellowes cranks the secrecy plot paradigm into overdrive, masterfully weaving together a dizzying number of secrecy plots. Will the rest of the family and the world learn of Mary's scandalous one-night stand and the removal of her paramour's dead body from her bedroom? Will the family discover that Edith's ward is really her illegitimate daughter? Did Bates kill his first wife because she tried to extort him? Not only each season but each episode takes us through the secrecy, revelation, reckoning, and recalibration stages of multiple characters.

Key Questions

The kinds of plotting questions I ask now have shifted in fascinating and productive ways. Rather than focus on issues of initiation and complication, plot points, or climaxes and denouements, I ask questions such as these:

Secret? What is the secret? Who knows it? What is at stake if the secret is discovered? Who can be hurt by its revelation? To what lengths will the protagonist or antagonist go to keep the secret hidden? What are the strategies of secret-keeping?

Revelation? Why and how is the secret revealed? Who reveals it? Is it confessed or does someone else extract the confession from the secret-keeper? Or is the secret discovered, and if so, who discovers it? Are there close calls or false revelations? Does the secret come out in stages? Who is most surprised and/or harmed by the revelation and why?

Reckoning? What are the immediate consequences of the revelation? Who delivers the reckoning, and who is reckoned with? When and where does this reckoning take place, and how do time and place inform the meaning of the reckoning? How much time elapses between the revelation and the reckoning? Is the reckoning physical, emotional, psychological, legal, ethical, or moral? Do the characters have to fully grapple with the consequences of this revelation? Have I spent too much time focused on the characters' maintenance of their secrets and failed to fully examine and dramatize the essential stages, the money scenes, in a secrecy plot—the revelations and reckonings?

Recalibration? What is learned from the revelation and reckoning? Who learns it? How are those involved in the secret changed, both short-term and long-term, by its revelation? Have I burdened my conclusion with a secrecy dump, à *la* Dickens, and not allowed my characters space to make sense of the transformations wrought by the revelations and reckonings?

These questions help me design a plot, figure out what I've done intuitively in a first draft, or diagnose the problems when my plots don't seem to be working effectively. I have learned, from analyzing classic and contemporary stories, novels, films, and plays, as well as my own work and thousands of student manuscripts over the years, that structural problems are almost always rooted in either the absence of one of these four stages of the secrecy plot ritual or mismanagement of the ritual itself.

Making It Personal

As a writer and as a creative writing teacher, I find this way of conceptualizing plot more valuable than conventional ways—for example, Freytag's triangle, the three-act structure of initiation-complication-resolution, cinematic plot points, the twelve stages of a hero's journey. Structure is linked organically to the revelatory ritual at the thematic center of all narrative explorations of character.

I'm fascinated by the drama and ethics of characters trying to keep or unmask secrets, and I often invest myself in characters who must wrestle with the moral dilemmas and burdens of their secrets or the secrets they expose in others. I think it's incumbent upon storytellers to examine the way secrecy figures into their lives and the lives of the characters they create. What is your relationship to this ritual of revelation? What kind of secrecy narratives are you drawn to—as a reader, as a consumer of narratives, as a person? That inquiry may tell you the kind of story you're intuitively attracted to and equipped to tell—and about which you may have something to say.

A Family Theme, a Family Secret

In addition to teaching a variety of undergraduate and graduate literary seminars and creative writing workshops, I also co-taught for many years an interdisciplinary literature and psychology course, Family Systems in Film and Literature. My co-instructor was Wayne Regina, a family systems theorist and therapist. In the course, we used stories, novellas, and films to illuminate the emotional legacies within families. In a family biography assignment, we asked students to write a narrative that examined a particular theme or secret within their own families. This assignment often provoked the most compelling, eloquent, and psychologically nuanced narratives I've read from students, even from students who don't consider themselves writers.

The assignment was so successful that I've adapted it for my fiction writing workshops, often with extraordinary results. I particularly like how the assignment encourages writers to move beyond simplistic depictions of characters (and families of characters) as victims and victimizers. Instead, it urges writers to examine the way a whole family contributes to a theme or secret, as well as the way that this theme or secret can clarify the identity, values, emotional history, desires, and anxieties of the family.

These considerations also deeply informed the writing and revision of several of my own books—*Last Call,* a short story cycle that depicts thirty years and three generations in the life of a West Texas family, and *The Girl from Charnelle,* a novel that focuses on a series of interlocking secrets in this same family, as well as stories and poems in my most recent collections—*Marrying Kind, Lost Soliloquies,* and *Love Songs for the Quarantined.*

A Family Theme

Predominant themes emerge over generations and are imprinted on a family as a kind of private mythology. "I come from a family of honorable thieves," a character might say. Or, as Nick Carraway announces at the beginning of *The Great Gatsby,* "My family have been prominent, well-to-do people in this middle-western city for three generations … and we have a tradition that we are descended from the Dukes of Buccleuch…."

Focus on a central theme in your fictional family's life. From where does this theme derive? How has this theme worked through the generations, positively and/or negatively? In what ways has it helped create a sense of loyalty and identity among the family members, or in what ways has it agitated the family's collective chronic anxiety and led to cut-off, regression, or reinvention? Keep in mind that with a family theme, the family members are often consciously and even *keenly* aware of the theme and its emotional legacy. Once you've established this theme, try one of the following narrative strategies.

Create a scene in which two characters from the family are at odds about the legitimacy of this family theme. Let one character attempt to convince the other to follow a destiny that will either reinforce or break free from this theme. Have the other character resist those arguments.

Or structure a story around three family members. Let one family member passionately attempt to convince a second (the protagonist perhaps) to follow or live by the family theme/legacy, and let a third member attempt to convince the second to resist, even undermine, the family theme/legacy. It helps to let the two members of the family who are trying to convince the protagonist have histories that reinforce their positions.

A Family Secret

According to family systems theory, there are no secrets within families. The entire family colludes, either consciously or unconsciously, in keeping and perpetuating a secret. Often a secret is linked to a family's conception of shame and may be used as a strategy for one generation to exert its will (about how to behave) over another generation. For example, in Maxine Hong Kingston's essay, "No Name Woman," the suppression of a Chinese woman's shame and suicide creates anxiety in her entire family, especially in her niece (Kingston herself) as she searches for "ancestral help" in defining her own identity. In James Baldwin's story, "Sonny's Blues," the narrator learns a terrible secret about his father and uncle that determines the way in which he tries to protect his brother.

Is there a secret in your fictional family? How has that secret generated either chronic or acute anxiety in the life of this family? Does that secret directly affect the story you wish to tell? Can you identify the members of this family who absorb or "bind" the anxiety of this suppressed secret? How do they bind it? What is the effect of the secret on the emotional health of the entire fictional family, as well as the individuals within it? Once you've explored the nuances of this secret, use it as the primary organizing strategy for your story. Here are two ways of doing this.

Start your story with a detailed accounting of the secret and then structure your narrative to dramatize the emotional effects of this secret on the character most affected—or "bound"—by the anxiety it creates.

Or structure your story as a mystery in which you create a protagonist who, from the beginning of the narrative, is on a search to discover the secret and who must contend with various family members' attempts to either aid or sabotage this search. A secret's power comes from its suppression, and there will always be members of a family who want either to continue the suppression of the secret or expose it in order to strip it of its emotional power.

Narrative Strategy and Dramatic Design

Arguably, the most difficult aspects of craft for writers to master are narrative strategy and dramatic design. When writers talk about dramatic or narrative structure, they often refer, either directly or indirectly, to one of six sources: Aristotle, Gustav Freytag, James Joyce, Northrop Frye, Joseph Campbell, or Syd Field. The Aristotelian model of dramatic structure, based on his analysis of Sophoclean tragedy, carries both an emotional and moral charge. It's all about the urgent, almost unbearable momentum generated by a tragedy, culminating in a reversal of fortune and a catharsis, a purging of pity and fear, for the audience. Gustav Freytag, in his famous pyramid, re-articulated Aristotle's pattern of action, drawing our attention to the initiation-complication-resolution pattern that dominates most narratives. Having the advantage of reading Shakespeare, Freytag expanded Aristotle's analysis into five distinct parts: exposition, rising action, climax, falling action, and denouement/catastrophe. Both Aristotle and Freytag were fascinated with and invested in examining the logistics of *plot*—the way that great texts keep readers and audiences in their grip.

For any film student, the dominant neo-Aristotelian structural paradigm was articulated by Syd Field in his popular series of *Screenplay* books (*The Screenwriter's Workbook* being the best). I know that I've got a film buff in my midst when the talk turns to three-act structures, plot points, midpoints, and pinches—essentially film language for Freytag's pyramid.

James Joyce—especially in the theories espoused by his alter-egos, Stephen Hero and later Stephen Dedalus—offered us our modern notion of the epiphanic story, a pattern of action that has a character begin in a state of innocence or mistaken belief, undergo some kind of experience that challenges that innocence, and end with behavioral change based on this newfound discovery. Often the discovery renders the protagonist temporarily (but productively) paralyzed, caught in a lyrical moment of intense awareness. These stories frequently end with an artful rendering of a new sensibility in which the soul of an object, of a character, of an experience seems suddenly to leap forth from behind an invisible mask and make itself radiant. The epiphanic cliché, which every workshop participant will recognize, is the story or poem or narrative essay that ends with some variation on "I suddenly realized" or "and then I discovered." It's a pattern so commonplace now that a writer as wonderfully attuned to the nuances of the epiphanic story as Charles Baxter was prompted to write an essay entitled "Against Epiphanies."

For those writers inherently drawn to archetypal notions of narrative patterning, the go-to critics are Northrop Frye, with his detailed study of genre conventions (romance, satire, tragedy, and comedy), and Joseph Campbell, with his even more elaborate articulation of the hero's journey. Frye is often a major eye-opener for young writers, especially when the genre conventions are expanded to include the pulpier conventions of mystery, Harlequin romance, horror, erotica, the Western, etc. Such examination prompts them to think more rigorously about the traditions of narrative that we so often take for granted. Joseph Campbell hardly needs any introduction to students. They grew up in a cultural milieu dominated by George Lucas and J. R. R. Tolkien (via Peter Jackson). In fact, I am no longer surprised by the number of twenty-year-old *Star Wars* and *Lord of the Rings* scholars who appear in my classes and who can recite, in alarmingly minute detail, the hero's epic trajectory from the Call to Adventure to the Return to the Ordinary World, and who have ambitions of writing their own sagas of Alderon and Middle Earth.

For writers particularly allergic to narrative, there is always the postmodern ethos of the erasure and self-conscious hyperawareness of narrative. Those who bring a postmodern antipathy or playfulness to their storytelling—a decidedly anti-narrative stance in which the goal seems to be the exposure of the artificiality of all narrative conventions—are, interestingly enough, the most sensitive to the dynamics of form and structure. Because postmodernism presupposes an understanding of the narrative traditions that have come before, these writers make form (and the limits of form) explicit in their texts. Postmodern writers and filmmakers often make readers and audiences feel as if we are studying an x-ray—which is simply another way of revealing what Joyce called the radiant "whatness" of experience.

When most of us read a story or novel, we desire two things: to be pulled through the narrative, to be held in its spell, and then to be able to reflect on the narrative as an aesthetic object that simultaneously harnesses and unleashes the deepest meanings of the text. Most of us want to experience that dynamic narrative motor that compels us to turn the pages or that has us chewing our nails in the theatre. But we also want to be able to consider the mysterious shape of the thing we just read or watched. We want to hold the whole novel, play, or film in our minds like a bejeweled golden egg. Narrative writing is a temporal art that moves characters through both time and the crucible of significant action. When we read a novel or see a play or film, we want the visceral moment-by-moment experience as well as the epiphanic experience of seeing the essential *whatness* of the narrative reveal itself. At its best, that essence has an aesthetically pleasing quality—a shape or form that, no matter how disturbing the subject matter, seems harmonious, organic, beautiful.

Narrative strategy is the first of these structural elements. It is a term to describe that dynamic, forward momentum—the tactics that a writer deploys to initiate, complicate, and resolve conflict and control the focus of a narrative. How does the writer make us care about or become invested in the characters' dilemmas? How does the writer create and release tension? Narrative strategy is intimately connected to these questions of plotting—to the way that action (what happens to characters, what characters do) energizes the experience of reading a text or seeing a performance. Narrative strategy is, I believe, particularly associated with the language of performing arts: action and reaction, tension and conflict, suspense and mystery, dread and laughter, initiation-complication-resolution. Aristotle, Freytag, and Field—all preoccupied with *staged* narratives—are especially concerned with these performative issues.

If narrative strategy is the way that the writer draws the reader into and through the story, then *dramatic design* is the underlying shape, form, or architecture of a story, often only recognized or understood in hindsight or after multiple readings. Design is intimately linked to theme—to the way structure informs and reinforces meaning. Dramatic design depends on the language of the visual, rather than performing, arts: form and pattern, symmetry and counterpoint, structure and architecture, foreground and background, perspective, balance, and harmony. Joyce, Campbell, and Frye—all interested in the ways in which narrative encodes and creates meaning—are theorists of dramatic design.

In the following pages, I'd like to explore five specific narrative strategies and dramatic design elements: secret identities, character-as-dramatist, multi-plot and thematic counterpoint, morality play/psychomachia, and rhyming action.

While I will refer to classic and contemporary fiction, plays, and films, I will concentrate my discussion on Shakespeare's *Othello*. Why *Othello*? It is a text that I can be reasonably sure most writers—of whatever genre—have read or seen performed. More importantly, Shakespeare is *the* master of both narrative strategy and dramatic design. And *Othello*, for my money, is the most contemporary, compelling, intimate, and disturbing of his great tragedies. It is also the play, Shakespearean scholars generally believe, that is the most perfectly constructed. Moreover, it offers equal insights for dramatists and writers of prose narrative because Shakespeare locates us, for most of the play, inside Iago's consciousness. Iago is, as I will suggest, the narrator of the play.

Secret Identities

I like to urge my students to create secret lives for their characters. Faulkner said that the only tale worth telling is the story of "the human heart in conflict with itself," a statement that implies a fundamental belief in the power of secret lives. Chekhov, in his great story, "The Lady with the Pet Dog," has his middle-aged protagonist Gurov realize that "through some strange, perhaps accidental, conjunction of circumstances, everything that was essential, of interest and value to him, everything in which he was sincere and did not deceive himself, everything that made the kernel of his life, was hidden from other people." This should be, I believe, a mantra for writers. My favorite novels, stories, and plays are often about secrecy and revelation. In fact, as I suggest in another essay in this collection, all plots are secrecy plots; every narrative is a ritual of revelation. Secrets yearn for revelation. Revelation provokes reckonings. And reckonings require emotional, psychological, legal, and spiritual recalibrations.

Shakespeare, I believe, understood this aspect of dramatic and narrative power more than any other writer. Every play has, at its center, a crucial misidentification of the characters. The plays focus on one or more of the characters disguising themselves in order to hide, to acquire what isn't theirs, to seek revenge, to be close to someone they love, or to unleash chaos. I can't think of a play that doesn't involve this strategy, and most of them focus on one or more of the characters purposefully creating alternative identities—either literally, as in those comedies in which the women dress up as young men, or metaphorically, as the characters create false perceptions of their real selves or resort to some other form of subterfuge. Rosalind, Portia, Viola, the Macbeths, Romeo and Juliet, Claudius, Hamlet, Polonius, Falstaff, Henry IV, Prince Hal, Edmund, Edgar. You name the play.

Most of the urgency and practically all of the dramatic irony in *Othello* derives from not only Iago's ability to create such a persuasive secret identity for himself ("I am not what I am"), but also from his ability to create persuasive alternative identities for all of the other characters. Iago is most certainly *not* "honest, honest Iago," though everyone else believes him to be. Moreover, he depicts Desdemona and Cassio as deceptive, mocking lovers—"as hot as goats, as prime as monkeys." Othello is not just the great Moorish general but, in Iago's mind, the man who has cuckolded him ("slipped between my sheets to do my office"), though there is no evidence to substantiate his claim.

The suspense of the play derives, in large part, from our desire to know if the secret identity of Iago as a villain will be revealed, if Othello will discover what is going on before the tragedy escalates, if Emilia will discover the truth about her husband, if Roderigo will rat out Iago.

Secrecy and revelation. This is, I believe, the primary dynamic—the crucial narrative strategy—in all of Shakespeare's plays. He is obsessed by it. It haunts his work. And it is one aspect of his art that perhaps most clearly accounts for his simultaneously enduring and disturbing power. We all live secret lives; Shakespeare masterfully animates that dilemma.

Character-as-Dramatist

As a writer, teacher, and occasional editor, one of the weaknesses that I feel undermines the work I read is the lack of agency in the characters. Frequently events happen *to* the characters, who perceive themselves to be victims of circumstance; fate is aligned against them. They primarily react rather than act. I often remind my students (and myself) to create characters who are culpable for their own actions. Let the characters get into and, if possible, cause the dilemmas that they must then work themselves out of.

Shakespeare apparently learned how to deal with this problem as he matured. Whereas his early plays often hinge on circumstance—*The Comedy of Errors*, for instance, or *Romeo and Juliet*—each of his mature works, especially the great tragedies, examines a protagonist who may be victimized by circumstances but ultimately takes responsibility for the consequences of those circumstances. Hamlet claims, "O curséd spite/That ever I was born to set [the situation] right," but his delays in carrying out the directive mandated by his father's ghost ultimately result in the deaths of all the major characters in the play. Macbeth seems to be a pawn of metaphysical forces—the witches, Lady Macbeth, the imaginary dagger that leads him on, the misleading prophecies—but at every stage, he makes a decision to act, to wade through the ocean of blood he has spilled. He is responsible for his actions; Macbeth's tragedy, as Ian McKellan (one of the great twentieth-century Macbeths) once said, is that "he is a killer with a conscience." Lear, too, sets in motion his own downfall by dividing his kingdom and requesting explicit expressions of affection from his daughters, disowning the one child who most loves him.

In *Othello,* Shakespeare does something very curious. He deliberately splits the focus of the drama. Although this is Othello's tragedy, Iago serves as *both* the antagonist and protagonist. This may be Othello's tragedy, but it is, as actors and directors know full well, Iago's play. Iago is Othello's antagonist, the villain, but he is also the one who manipulates all the characters and serves literally as the narrator and dramatic architect for the action. Except for Hamlet, no character in Shakespeare has as many lines as Iago. Shakespeare invites us to watch and interpret the action of the play primarily through Iago's consciousness.

Repeatedly, in soliloquy after soliloquy and aside after aside, he steps forward and shares his evolving "plot to ensnare them all."

Iago's plan energizes the narrative. We hear him devise it, and then we watch, in horror and fascination, as he executes it, brilliantly modifying and improvising along the way. Shakespeare forces us to root for *and* against Iago. The great Edwardian literary critic, A. C. Bradley, argued that the peculiarly disturbing power of *Othello* is due to what he called its "plot of incubation." We become co-conspirators in the genesis of Iago's plan, and then we watch as it transforms into the monstrosity that destroys all the characters. We are horrified in part because Shakespeare has made us Iago's confidants. There is, in fact, a long theatrical history of audience members shouting warnings to Othello and Desdemona about Iago—a comic spectacle that nevertheless suggests the almost unbearable moral complexity with which Shakespeare enmeshes not just his characters but his audience.

Like Richard III, Hamlet, the bastard Edmund in King Lear, and Prospero, Iago is an expert dramatist, a "plotter." He is, in fact, the most multi-talented of all of Shakespeare's great character-dramatists. Iago is also the lead actor, director, choreographer, and improviser, taking advantage of every opportunity that presents itself, most notably with Desdemona's handkerchief.

One of Iago's primary dramatic methods is to create little plays within the play. Anyone even casually familiar with Shakespeare's work will realize that the play-within-a-play device is one of his pet narrative strategies. We see it in the histories (especially the tavern scenes in *Henry IV, Part One*) and in the comedies. In *Hamlet*, Polonius and Claudius plot to eavesdrop on Hamlet; Hamlet in turn concocts his mousetrap scheme, through the use of the traveling players, in order to "catch the conscience of the king." This play-within-a-play strategy is a crucial source of energy in Shakespeare's work, usually serving as the dramatic center of the plays, performing exceedingly well on stage. It also provides what we might call a pre-postmodern commentary on the action itself: we are spectators watching a drama in which characters comment on the drama they have created.

Othello is one grand play-within-a-play. Iago constructs dumb shows and mini-plays—either in the stories he tells Roderigo and Othello (about Cassio's incriminating dreams, about the misplaced handkerchief, about the sex between Desdemona and Cassio), or in the mini-plays he actually stages, most notably in the scene where Othello is "encaved" as a secret audience member while Iago makes Cassio unwittingly indict himself. Iago emerges as Shakespeare's definitive, albeit most sinister, portrait of the artist. At the end of the tragedy, like a good artist (like Shakespeare himself, in fact), Iago refuses to explain his work: "What you know you know," he tells Othello, who demands some explanation for why his ensign has "ensnared [his] body and soul." "From this time forth will I never speak word," Iago icily responds. In the final moments, the nobleman Lodovico, like a moralizing reviewer, forces Iago and the audience to "look on the tragic loading of this bed." He tells Iago, "This is thy work. The object poisons sight."

For Lodovico—and for many audiences and readers—Iago becomes a dramatist of gratuitous violence. The tableau of the dead Desdemona, Emilia, and Othello on the bed is not simply a "tragic loading" but evidence of what Lynda E. Boose, in "Let It Be Hid: The Pornographic Aesthetic in *Othello*," claims is the pornographic nature of Iago's imagination and of *Othello* itself. Iago is not just a psychological portrait of evil, Boose asserts, with a clearly defined motive for malignancy, but rather he "is a *strategy* for luring members of the audience into complicity with his project and into confrontation with their own prurience."

I am not suggesting by this analysis of the character-as-dramatist that we all go out and yoke our narratives to our villains, that we spawn a thousand Iagos. I am, however, suggesting that in *Othello* Shakespeare provides us with a brilliant model for how to energize our stories by allowing our protagonists to do the plotting for us—to let them conceive plans and then attempt to carry out those plans, encouraging the reader and audience to participate, however uncomfortably, as confidants in the dramatic unfolding.

Multi-Plot and Thematic Counterpoint

There is, as you may realize by now, a considerable gray area between narrative strategy and dramatic design. While Shakespeare's secret-identity and character-as-dramatist structures are more clearly, to my mind, narrative strategies, serving as the engines of plot, they also have thematic implications. If your stories or scripts deal obsessively with characters purposefully cloaking their identities or creating alternative identities for other characters, then the stories you write will be, whether you realize it or not, about betrayal, revelation, and the consequences of a secret life. If you choose a point of view that privileges a character who has the most agency, rather than a character to whom events happen, then you are making not only a narrative statement but also a philosophical one about complicity and moral responsibility. But having said that, secret identities and the character-as-dramatist are closer on the continuum to narrative strategy than they are to dramatic design. These are deliberate methods to energize a narrative and to create tension and suspense.

The next structural method that I'll discuss—multi-plot and thematic counterpoint—exists in the gray zone between narrative strategy and dramatic design.

Shakespeare habitually uses his subplots and secondary characters to inform, counterpoint, and comment thematically on the main plot and the protagonist's dilemma. We see it most effectively in the contrast between the court, tavern, and battlefield scenes in the *Henry IV* plays, the upstairs/downstairs dynamics of *Twelfth Night*, the world of the fairies, the lovers, and the "mechanicals" in *A Midsummer Night's Dream*, and the fully developed Lear/Gloucester double plot of *King Lear*. We also see it in the contrast between the three avenging sons—Hamlet, Laertes, and Fortinbras—in *Hamlet*. It is a process of narrative construction that operates by comparison and contrast.

Othello, like *Macbeth*, is one of the more streamlined of Shakespeare's plays. Yet even so, we can see the way that Shakespeare weaves together his subplots and uses his secondary characters so that they comment on Othello's predicament.

Let me focus, for the sake of expediency, on the most prevalent example. *Othello*—the whole play—is Shakespeare's synonym for sexual jealousy. *Othello* is, in fact, the most well-known text in all of literature that examines and depicts the corrosive effects of jealousy. Even those who do not know the play can probably paraphrase if not recite its most famous lines: "O, beware, my lord, of jealousy!/It is the green-eyed monster, which doth mock/The meat it feeds on." The central plot involves Iago persuading Othello that Desdemona and Cassio are lovers. And yet, in typical Shakespearean multi-plot fashion, that is not the only variation on the theme of jealousy and betrayal. Almost every character is consumed, on one level or another, by jealousy. Although there are volumes of criticism devoted to the reason for Iago's malignant behavior, Shakespeare lets Iago rather unambiguously articulate his reasons. Iago tells the audience that he's seeking revenge against the Moor primarily because there are rumors that Othello has slept with Emilia. He doesn't know if the rumors are true, but he will act as if they are. Later, and even more outlandishly, Iago "suspects Cassio with [his] nightcap too."

The minor characters are also motivated by jealousy. Roderigo has been driven mad by his desire for Desdemona; Iago manipulates him by vividly suggesting the sexual relationship between Desdemona and Othello and then later Desdemona and Cassio. Bianca, the courtesan who has fallen in love with Cassio, flies into a rage when she thinks Cassio has given her the handkerchief of another lover. Desdemona's father, Brabantio, behaves more like a spurned lover (awakened from his dream of Desdemona making love to the Moor by the shouts that "an old black ram is tupping [his] white ewe") than a betrayed father, culminating in his warning to Othello: "Beware, Moor, she has betrayed me and may thee." Even the political context of the play reinforces these thematic correspondences; the Venetian Senate dispatches Othello to Cypress because they fear the Turks are on their way to seize the prized (and in this play, feminized) isle of Cypress.

The play is designed to reveal a complicated network of interlocking erotic triangles—a structure that is prevalent in the comedies and romances but rare in the tragedies. In this play, the triangle of Othello/Desdemona/Cassio is offset by a dizzying array of other emotional triangles that include Iago/Emilia/Othello, Othello/Desdemona/Iago, Iago/Emilia/Cassio, Brabantio/Desdemona/Othello, Iago/Othello/Cassio (a relationship that is often performed with a homoerotic subtext), and Bianca/Cassio/"the lewd minx" who Bianca believes gave Cassio the handkerchief.

Shakespeare's method is both to build tension and create meaning through these correspondences and thematic counterpoints. He shows us Othello's problem through a prism of thematically and dramatically linked subplots. This prism both governs our way of reading the play and also subverts thematic certainty.

We judge Othello's behavior toward Desdemona, and his descent into jealousy-induced madness, by comparing and contrasting his behavior to that of the other characters—especially the other triangulated lovers—who also "love not wisely but too well." Iago responds to the unfounded rumors of Emilia and Othello's affair with a cold, calculating rage. Roderigo is transformed into a simpering and gullible dupe, willing to do anything—sell his lands, offer up his riches to Iago, follow the wars, incite a mutiny, and kill an officer—in order to sleep with the woman to whom he unreasonably believes he's entitled. Brabantio's fears and enraged call for justice deteriorate into a grief that, we learn in the final lines, has killed him. Bianca's jealousy ignites her anger against Cassio and leaves her helpless to do anything about it but rail against her lover in the streets. Emilia's belief that Iago has cheated on her renders her overly eager to please him (e.g., filching Desdemona's handkerchief for her husband) and yet also plants the seeds of her pragmatic feminism, as she encourages Desdemona in their final scene together to envision a world in which women are equals to their male counterparts, entitled to the same pleasures, privileges, vices, and faults as their husbands: "Then let them use us well; else let them know,/ The ills we do, their ills instruct us so."

While the characters respond differently to these jealous impulses, in each case the jealousy diminishes them, leaving them disconnected from their best selves, enraged or gullible, blinded by passion, bereft of coherent access to language, and prey to an insidious insecurity or bitterness that indeed does mock the meat it feeds on.

This method of using secondary characters and subplots to counterpoint Othello's plight is one of the primary ways that Shakespeare weaves magic into the web of his design. As both a narrative strategy and a dramatic design, multi-plot and thematic counterpoint is far from being particular to Shakespeare's art. Anyone who has enjoyed the novels of Austen, Dickens, Tolstoy, George Eliot, John Irving, Richard Russo, Jane Smiley, Salmon Rushdie, or Zadie Smith, or films such as *Nashville, Gosford Park, Magnolia, Boogie Nights, Crash,* or *Babel,* or television series such as *The West Wing, ER, Deadwood, Mad Men,* or *Downton Abbey* can appreciate the narrative and dramatic power of multi-plot and thematic counterpoint. It's difficult, in fact, to conceive of the multi-plot structure of today's novels, plays, films, or television shows without the complexity and brilliance of Shakespeare's example.

Morality Play and Psychomachia

Renaissance drama's immediate aesthetic ancestors were the morality plays, still very popular in England in Shakespeare's childhood and adolescence, and a model of narrative that has never really disappeared. The morality play is simply a struggle between two forces, Vice and Virtue (a bad angel and a good angel), for the soul of the protagonist, an Everyman or Everywoman.

Shakespeare relied upon—and often radically subverted—this structure throughout his career, most obviously in the *Henry IV* plays (Henry IV and Falstaff vying for Prince Hal's political soul) and *The Tempest* (Caliban and Ariel as Prospero's good and bad angels, both of whom he must "acknowledge"). As Marjorie Garber, one of the best and most accessible contemporary Shakespearean critics, suggests in *Shakespeare After All*:

> Othello pits Iago on one side and Desdemona on the other, the two contending for the possession, in the sense of property or ownership and also that of magical or demonic enchantment, of Othello. Iago is in many ways a more sophisticated version of the medieval Vice, that stock character who was a figure of consummate evil and anarchy, whose purpose was to coax the hero into sin.

Yet, while Shakespeare intentionally uses the simple morality play design in *Othello* as his substructure, the play is a far more sophisticated examination of moral and psychological conflict. "Another way," Garber continues,

> of understanding this same dramatic situation—a tug-of-war with Othello in the center—is to see both Iago and Desdemona as reflecting aspects of Othello's own mind. In this case the psychomachia (literally, 'struggle of the soul') is taking place *within* him, and the contest he undergoes is a

struggle of conflicting impulses, creative or sexual, anarchic or destructive.

I need not elaborate here on the complexity with which Shakespeare develops this structure in this play. I only wish to point out that Shakespeare uses the morality play/psychomachia design to help us navigate our way through the play. This morality play design mitigates some of the distress we naturally feel in the claustrophobic company of Iago's psychopathology. The design provides a safe haven for us, a way to balance the compelling narrative strategy of having Iago as our narrator/dramatist. Unlike the other characters in the play, we are under no delusion about Iago's moral affiliations. We may, for the two-hour traffic of this play, be his confidant, but the play is structured in such a way so that we understand that we're clearly in the company of a brilliant and charismatic devil.

One might wonder if the morality play/psychomachia design is a relic of the past—a structure more relevant for a religious rather than a secular literature. I think not. We see this structure prevalent in not only Shakespeare's plays but in prose narratives from *The Pilgrim's Progress* to Hawthorne's novels and stories ("Young Goodman Brown," *The Scarlet Letter*), to Joseph Conrad's fiction. We see it touted in the strenuous polemics of writer/teacher John Gardner; he began his career as a Medievalist who, despite being one of the most interesting postmodernists, urged writers and readers not to abandon the traditional imperatives of literature: to entertain and to morally instruct. And this morality play/psychomachia design is clearly embedded in the structure of *Moby-Dick, The Great Gatsby,* and *All the King's Men,* as well as numerous films, from *Star Wars* to *Platoon* to *Lord of the Rings.* Joseph Campbell's hero's journey, which he claimed was a cross-cultural pattern that has been around since the dawn of narrative, is in essence an elaboration on the morality play/psychomachia design. There is always going to be a struggle for our souls; the writer's job is to find ways to dramatize that struggle.

Rhyming Action

The last element of dramatic design I want to discuss is what Charles Baxter, in *Burning Down the House,* calls "rhyming action"—internal structural rhyme, encoded in the dramatic shape of the scenes, which gives the reader (or audience member) the sense that the narrative is not only moving forward in time but also repeating an aesthetically beautiful pattern of action. "It's customary to talk about effective language or effective dramatic structure," Baxter says,

> but almost no one ever talks about beautiful action.... I mean actions that feel aesthetically correct and just—actions or dramatic images that cause the hair on the back of our necks to stand

up, as if we were reading a poem. My conclusion is that it often has to do with dramatic repetition, or echo effects. I think of this as rhyming action.

Shakespeare brings his poet's sensibility to the construction of his plays. He uses these narrative echoes to give shape, focus, and resonance to his plots. There are far too many examples of rhyming action in Shakespeare's plays to note here, but let me elaborate on the most dominant example in *Othello*. For me, one of the most ingenious and disturbing aspects of this tragedy is that it links the world of marriage and sexual infidelity to the world of criminal investigation and jurisprudence. It connects, in other words, a seemingly objective sphere of dispassionate law to the passionate emotionality of the bedroom. That link is encoded not only in the language of the play but in the actual design of each scene and act.

The first act, which I think of as "Othello's Defense," begins with Iago and the spurned Roderigo waking Desdemona's father to warn him that Othello, the "old black ram," has "stolen" Brabantio's "white ewe," and they are even now "making the beast with two backs." Brabantio seeks out Othello, and they both proceed to the Senate, where the Duke and the other senators are preparing for war. Brabantio publicly accuses Othello of bewitching Desdemona and demands an immediate trial. Othello testifies in his defense, and then Desdemona is summoned for her testimony. Ultimately, the Duke and senators, as a mock court, render a verdict of innocence, and the couple is sent on their quasi-honeymoon to Cypress, where the Turks are expected to invade.

In this opening act, Shakespeare establishes the pattern of action that will rhyme in the subsequent acts, a pattern that looks like this: Alarm→ Accusation→ Investigation→ Testimony & Evidence→ Verdict→Justice & Punishment.

Act Two, which I think of as "Mutiny on Cypress," focuses on Iago's attempts to discredit Cassio and to have him stripped of his lieutenancy—a position Iago feels should rightfully be his. In the long, pivotal scene in this act, this whole pattern is repeated. Iago gets Cassio drunk and enlists Roderigo to start a fight with him. When Cassio chases after Roderigo and then begins to quarrel with the governor of the isle, Iago sounds the alarms, screams mutiny, and awakens Othello, who, enraged, holds a quick inquiry in which Iago is forced to testify against Cassio. Othello strips Cassio of his rank and leaves Iago in charge of restoring order and consoling the despondent and punished Cassio.

Acts Three and Four might be subtitled "Beware, My Lord, of Jealousy" and "Give Me the Ocular Proof," and again Shakespeare repeats the pattern. Iago artfully slanders Desdemona, encouraging Othello to "look to your wife" and to be wary of "the green-eyed monster." Through insinuation, Iago builds his case against Desdemona and Cassio, driving Othello insane until Othello appoints Iago as his lieutenant and they plot to murder the adulterous couple. Act Four dramatizes Othello's preliminary interrogation of Desdemona and Emilia. Perplexed, Othello then accuses Iago of lying and demands that Iago "prove my love a whore" with tangible, conclusive evidence—what he calls "the ocular proof." Iago builds his case more persuasively, fabricating circumstantial evidence, using the handkerchief as his main piece of evidence, perjuring himself outrageously in his description of Cassio's confessions, and then creating the dumb show in which Cassio apparently confesses in front of Othello to his affair with Desdemona.

Act Five is the final execution of Iago's plan, an act that I refer to as "The Cause," and a final iteration of this ritual of jurisprudence. Iago plans to use Roderigo to kill off Cassio, and that scene ends with Iago murdering Roderigo, shouting "treason," and then setting up a mock trial to implicate Bianca in the attempted murder of Cassio. Meanwhile, Othello prepares himself like a judge and executioner to sacrifice Desdemona because, if he doesn't, "she'll betray more men." Othello's rationalized, impartial justice deteriorates in the bedroom as Desdemona, on her deathbed, refuses to confess to a crime she didn't commit. Othello strangles her. Emilia arrives, realizes the truth of the situation, and begins to publicly decry this murder and her husband's complicity. Othello is arrested. A mini-trial ensues in the bedroom, during which Emilia interrogates Iago, and the noblemen who have been called forth attempt to ferret out the truth of this calamity. By the end of the play, Iago kills his wife and is sentenced to be tortured. Othello confesses to his crime, takes responsibility for it, and stabs himself, in effect serving as both the convicted perpetrator and his own executioner.

In each of these acts, an alarm is sounded and characters are awakened—presumably from sleep. In each instance, the alarm announces a criminal action—theft, mutiny, betrayal, slander, treason, and murder. In each act, those who are called to action respond with inquiries, investigations, and interrogations. That activity is followed by impromptu judicial proceedings: Brabantio rushing to retrieve his abused "ewe," and then to the Senate to plead his case; Othello investigating the drunken mutiny, soliciting testimony from Iago, and then punishing Cassio; Iago accusing his general's wife of infidelity and then having to substantiate the charge; Iago prosecuting Bianca; Emilia calling for justice, the noblemen apprehending Othello, Othello confessing and then killing himself; and Iago sentenced and forced to look upon the poisoned tableau he has wrought.

This pattern of Alarm→ Accusation→ Investigation→ Testimony & Evidence→ Verdict → Justice & Punishment is the rhyming action that mimics the entire judicial process, like a Renaissance version of *Law & Order*.

In the first iterations, Iago causes the false alarms and creates the chaos and false allegations and unjustified punishments. But in the final scene, Emilia sounds the alarm, issues the accusations, and testifies against her husband. She is punished by Iago for her marital "treason." Her testimony, however, does lead to the public revelation of the truth, the rendering of justice, and the promise of punishment for both her husband and Othello.

To further emphasize the poetic nature of this rhyming action, it's worth noting that in the first and last episodes, Iago's plans are foiled, but in the middle acts (I'm counting Acts Three and Four as one long example of the pattern), he succeeds and his plot is advanced. There is a kind of natural symmetry to this action—an ABBA pattern that is as aesthetically pleasing to the reader and the audience member as the formal components of a sonnet or a villanelle are to the reader of poetry. What Shakespeare has done here is to encode—in the very rhyming structure of his acts—a sense of form as well as a subtle narrative promise that moral order will be restored.

One might suggest that this rhyming action is less an example of dramatic design than an example of narrative strategy since it is so tightly bound up with the construction of acts and scenes. It is certainly a method by which

Shakespeare generates suspense and tension in addition to creating the "beautiful action" that Charles Baxter describes as making the hairs on the back of our necks stand up. Of course, such an argument is convincing. While I've attempted here to parse the differences between narrative strategy and dramatic design, the two are inextricably linked. An effective narrative strategy *should* reinforce the deepest themes of the story or play. And dramatic design can easily provide a method for generating suspense as well as serve as a structure for encoding meaning.

Rhyming action, at least as it operates in *Othello*, illustrates just how intentionally Shakespeare controlled the focus of the play and how he used design as a way to explore the tension and tragedy that results when two juxtaposed spheres of experience—the sphere of rational justice and the sphere of unexamined sexual jealousy—collide. The play's deepest concerns are contained inside that violent collision of the rational and the emotional. In this way, form is organically tied to content. Form, in fact, *is* meaning.

"Immature poets borrow; mature poets steal," T. S. Eliot famously claimed. What I think he meant was that apprentice writers of all genres tend to focus on and imitate the surface beauty of the writing they most admire—style, syntax, diction, dialogue, a tone or philosophical stance.

The experienced writer, by contrast, engages in an assiduous study of form, of structure, of the patterns of connection that help a writer transform the chaos of experience into a work of art. While the narrative strategies and design elements I've discussed here may at first seem peculiar to Shakespeare's plays in general and to *Othello* in particular, my hope is that they are more broadly applicable to any narrative, and that they offer short story writers, novelists, narrative poets, and nonfiction writers, as well as playwrights and screenwriters, some possibilities for exploring the way stories are made and the meaning that emerges from that construction.

The Cyclical Imagination: Short Story Cycles, Linked Stories, and Novels-in-Stories

We are all hard-wired not just for narrative but for *cyclical* narrative—a compulsive need for stories that are both self-contained and interdependent. We see this need expressed in the ancient Greek tragedies and epics, Chaucer's *Canterbury Tales* and Shakespeare's history plays, and in modernist classics such as Sherwood Anderson's *Winesburg, Ohio* and Earnest Hemingway's *In Our Time*. We see it today in our fascination with television dramas, sitcoms, and reality shows, and in the film industry's love affair with sequels and franchises. We see it in the literature for children and young adults, from C. S. Lewis' *The Chronicles of Narnia* to Lemony Snicket's *A Series of Unfortunate Events,* as well as the phenomenal international success of J. K. Rowling's *Harry Potter* and Suzanne Collins' *Hunger Games* series. We see it in most genre literature, and in our attraction to such serial protagonists as Sherlock Holmes, Miss Marple, and Philip Marlowe, as well as Kinsey Millhone and Easy Rawlings.

As a child, I was hooked on the Encyclopedia Brown and Tarzan series, and as a student and now a writer and professor, I've been equally enthralled with the cyclical narratives devoted to Oedipus and his daughters, Prince Hal, Sherlock Holmes, and Rabbit Angstrom, not to mention *The West Wing, Deadwood, Mad Men, Breaking Bad, The Americans, Downton Abbey, The Handmaid's Tale*, and the intricately mosaic films of Robert Altman, Quentin Tarantino, Rodrigo Garcia, Krzysztof Kieślowski, and Guillermo Arriaga.

For the last couple of decades, I have taught a course for advanced undergraduate and graduate students on short story cycles—part study of literary form, part fiction workshop—in which I make the argument for cyclical and mosaic narrative design and help writers understand the formal options available to them.

The short story cycle is particularly well suited for storytellers who want to make the leap from writing stories to writing book-length narrative fiction. It's equally compelling for the novelist who wants to work in new ways and yearns to take advantage of the short story cycle's natural reliance on mosaic design and a non-linear aesthetic. It's also ideal for serious readers—not to mention fiction writers, poets, and nonfiction writers—who want to understand the renaissance of the short story cycle and its impact on other narrative and non-narrative genres. It's ideal for those writers and readers who want to immerse themselves in what I think of as the cyclical imagination.

What's in a Name?

Short story cycle, linked stories, novel-in-stories, ring of stories, circle of stories, interlocking stories, story sequence, unified story collection, composite novel, short story novel. What are these things, and why can't we decide on a name for them? Does the confusion surrounding the name suggest the form's lack of identity, or does it reflect its vitality as a hybrid form? How do short story cycles—and the stories and/or chapters within them—resemble and differ from more traditional collections of stories? How do they resemble and differ from novels? What expectations does the writer create for the reader by announcing that a collection of stories is a cycle, or a ring of stories, or a novel-in-stories, or even a novel?

The short story cycle has a longer and, in some ways, more deeply entrenched tradition than the novel. It stretches at least as far back as Boccaccio's *The Decameron,* which inspired Chaucer's *Canterbury Tales.* We see the form alive in *A Thousand and One Nights* with Scheherazade's artful storytelling serving as her means of self-preservation—a meta-story linking each of her tales. The form flourished in the nineteenth century and early twentieth century with the serialization of novels, from Dickens to Henry James, and with Arthur Conan Doyle's *The Adventures of Sherlock Holmes,* and took on new life in Russia with Turgenev, writers who inspired many of the great early European and American modernists.

In 1914, James Joyce's *Dubliners*—with its focus on place, its depiction of a variety of Dublin inhabitants, its consistent theme of isolation, and its intricate progression of consciousness from youth to middle age—established a new standard for how a collection of stories could be unified, and how it might be read as a unified collection, with a coherent (though not linear) design and integrity. Only a few years later, in America, the middle-aged novelist and short story writer, Sherwood Anderson, also used place and community as the central organizing principle of his masterpiece, but created an even more intricate narrative design and announced to the world that his *Winesburg, Ohio* ushered in a new method of storytelling: "It's my form," he cheerfully boasted. "I invented it." In reality, Anderson and Joyce merely revitalized an old form, drawing upon the story cycle's insistence on the simultaneous existence of both parts *and* wholes—a form that seemed to perfectly embody the modernist preoccupation with subjectivity, de-centered narratives, and regional particularity.

Most of the great American fiction writers of the first half of the twentieth century considered Joyce and Anderson literary forefathers. Hemingway, William Faulkner, F. Scott Fitzgerald, John Steinbeck, and Katherine Anne Porter, to name only a few, would all return again and again to the short story cycle form for their own collections. The aesthetic bar had been raised. Joyce and Anderson would also foster, with their work, a deep affinity for the cyclical imagination, which would define, to some extent, all of these other writers' work, none more so than Faulkner, who perceived early in his career that each story and book he wrote could be part of one long, interconnected narrative—the emotional, intellectual, psychological, and moral history of his imaginary Yoknapatawpha County, what he referred to as his "little postage stamp of native soil."

The story cycle form continued to flourish after World War II and throughout the rest of the twentieth century, finding new expressions in the work of Bernard Malamud, J. D. Salinger, Isaac Bashevis Singer, John Updike, Philip Roth, Joyce Carol Oates, Grace Paley, Alice Munro, Russell Banks, Tim O'Brien, Susan Minot, Garrison Keillor, Charles Baxter, Jennifer Egan, Elizabeth Strout, and Joan Silber. Minorities, women, and first- and second-generation immigrants have discovered that the short story cycle's dual effect of both separation and integration speaks profoundly to their multicultural experience and to the sense of non-linear, mosaic design in their own lives. From the early 1980s on, we experienced in America yet another renaissance in story cycles that includes work by Louise Erdrich, Gloria Naylor, Amy Tan, Bharati Mukherjee, Edward P. Jones, Sherman Alexie, Cristina Garcia, Jhumpa Lahiri, Edwidge

Danticat, Junot Diaz, among others. In his study of the form, *The Contemporary American Short-Story Cycle: The Ethnic Resonance of Genre,* James Nagel argues,

> But never has the genre of the short-story cycle been used with greater force or variety than in the American fiction of the 1980s and 1990s, when it became the genre of choice for emerging writers from a variety of ethnic and economic backgrounds. These authors have created works with ideological force and impressive artistic richness, establishing a legacy that needs to be explored not only in general terms but with a detailed examination of some of the exemplary volumes that are representative of the contemporary short story cycle.

On the most basic level, short story cycles are not quite novels, and yet their effect is greater than that of self-contained stories because the stories within them must stand alone and also be interdependent, allowing (or forcing) the writer to extend a character's trajectory or expand a thematic idea beyond the narrative limitations of the story. The story cycle speaks not only to our modernist penchant for subjective exploration of consciousness or to our postmodern fascination with unstable or fractured narratives. It also satisfies our desire to resist dichotomies—to insist upon parts *and* wholes, complete *and* provisional closure, narrative energy *and* lyrical stillness, self-containment *and* interconnection, independence *and* community. As Michael Chabon said, in a review of John Updike's *Too Far to Go,* a short story cycle about the decades-long tumultuous relationship between a married couple, "A group of linked narratives can create an effect you can't get from a novel or from one story alone. It's like a series of snapshots taken over time. Part of the pleasure is turning to them again and again. The interest lies in what has happened in the interstices."

The Case for Story Cycles

Before making a case for why you should, if you are a fiction writer, write a short story cycle, let me make the case for why you *shouldn't* embark on such an endeavor. Pulitzer Prize-winning novelist Richard Russo—best known for his long, intricately plotted Dickensian epics set in Maine and upstate New York—suggested years ago, in a letter to me when he was my graduate school mentor, three theories for what may be called "the current rash" of short story cycles:

> Some might say that the story cycle is the perfect genre for a writer who can't plot a novel; a series of stories would be more manageable, less daunting, requiring less courage. Others might say that the story cycle's popularity is due to the proliferation of creative writing workshops, which favor the story over the novel for the simple reason that a story can be discussed and evaluated in a short time, and

a series of them can be viewed both singly and as a group. Still others might point a finger at cynical publishers who know that story cycles can often be published as novels, which almost always sell far better than collections of short fiction.

Practitioners, readers, and teachers of the form at least intuitively understand that there is validity to each argument. Yet let me suggest counter-arguments.

Yes, the creative writing workshop *does* favor the story over the novel. The workshop method, as American writing programs practice it, is a finely nuanced mechanism for making sure a story is self-contained, and a series of them can be viewed, as Russo suggested, "both singly and as a group." Since most aspiring writers at some point will find themselves in a workshop situation, why not take advantage of the inherent strength of this form and leverage it to your advantage as you write your first book? The short story cycle is, as Antonya Nelson, winner of the Rea Award for her lifetime achievement as a short story writer, suggests, "a nice bridge between writing stories and writing novels. It works well because you can present one story in the point of view of one character in a family, then another from somebody else's point of view. This gives you the position, as a writer, of wandering through the house and observing everybody's relationship." For the apprentice writer, still learning his or her craft, it's important to be challenged to work on a whole book rather than just miscellaneous stories. And a writer's first story cycle sometimes turns out to be a major artistic accomplishment, occasionally even a writer's signature work, as was the case with Amy Tan's *The Joy Luck Club*.

Why not partner with publishers? Most fiction writers want a wide readership, and everyone knows that novels almost always sell far better than short story collections; in fact, miscellaneous collections of stories, unless packaged with a novel in a two-book deal, are notoriously difficult to sell to commercial publishers. Most short story collections published today are at least thematically linked. And many story cycles are actually published as novels (*Love Medicine, The Joy Luck Club,* Harriet Doerr's *Stones for Ibarra,* Jennifer Egan's *A Visit from the Goon Squad,* Joan Silber's *Improvement*), or novels-in-stories (Justin Cronin's *Mary and O'Neil,* Adam Braver's *Mr. Lincoln's Wars,* Elizabeth Strout's Pulitzer Prize-winning *Olive Kitteridge*), or more vaguely as "works of fiction" (Tim O'Brien's *The Things They Carried,* Susan Minot's *Monkeys,* and Melissa Banks' *The Girls' Guide to Hunting and Fishing*). Perhaps this kind of marketing subterfuge, if you want to call it that, *is* cynical, but my guess is it suggests that editors, publishers, and readers naturally yearn for books that at least *seem* interconnected, books in which the whole is greater than the sum of its parts.

And sometimes the very act of calling a short story cycle a novel challenges and enlarges the reader's conception of form, as many of the titles above reveal and that a "novel" like Jennifer Egan's Pulitzer Prize-winning *A Visit from the Goon Squad* epitomizes—with its radical experiments in form, its loose-knit weave of characters, its militant non-linearity, and its emphasis on thematic rather than narrative unity.

It's also crucial to emphasize that the story cycle form, while invaluable to the apprentice, is not just a beginner's form. You don't graduate from one form to another. It has its own literary history, formal integrity, and aesthetic challenges. Many of the best cycles—*Winesburg, Ohio*, Updike's *Too Far to Go*, O'Brien's *The Things They Carried*, Butler's *A Good Scent from a Strange Mountain*, Strout's *Olive Kitteridge*, Silber's *Ideas of Heaven* and multiple-award-winning *Improvement*, Egan's *Goon Squad*—are written by established novelists searching for a new method of storytelling.

Ultimately, the short story cycle allows writers to release themselves from the constraints of linear logic, what Madison Smartt Bell calls, in his perceptive book on form in fiction, *Narrative Design*, "those chains of cause and effect, strings of dominoes always falling forward." The story cycle *is* the perfect form for writers who can't (or don't wish to) concentrate on plot. The desire to minimize plot doesn't necessarily imply a failure of either ability or artistic courage. The story cycle, as a subgenre, is characterized primarily by modular or mosaic design.

As Bell suggests, "linear narrative design is primarily a subtractive process: cutting away extraneous elements in service of the overall structure. The writer is like a carver or sculptor, chiseling away dross to cleanly and clearly reveal the narrative vectors of action." Such a writer thinks of "narrative as motion (characters moving through time), with psychological cause and effect" serving as the primary agents of tension, conflict, and suspense. By contrast, "modular design," Bell continues, "is primarily an additive process: the writer is more like a mosaicist, assembling fragments that can be understood, at a greater distance, as a coherent, shapely design."

Symmetry, balance, counterpoint, rhyming action, and composition serve as the basic strategies for the writer who works with modular or mosaic design. The story cycle can be thought of as a geometrical shape rather than a streamlined narrative or dramatic process. This approach to storytelling liberates the writer from the linear logic of cause and effect, and it allows greater freedom for the writer to improvise around a substructure the way a jazz musician riffs around the melody.

The beauty of the short story cycle is that it can, at its most sophisticated, simultaneously provide the pleasures of *both* linear and mosaic design. One approach does not preclude the other, which accounts for the peculiar power and sense of mystery that we often feel while reading a good story cycle. We may believe—after finishing Alice Munro's *The Beggar Maid* or Edwidge Danticat's *The Dew Breaker* or Blanche McCrary Boyd's little known but exquisite *The Revolution of Little Girls*—that the linear logic of most novels seems suddenly irrelevant, even impotent.

Unifying Strategies

How do you go about consciously designing and writing a short story cycle? While there are many ways, both overt and subtle, to unify a short story cycle, and while the best cycles employ a variety of unifying strategies rather than just one overarching strategy, it is useful, I believe, to examine the primary unifying strategies and to envision these strategies as existing on a continuum, with some leaning more toward the traditional collection of unlinked stories while others lean toward the narrative coherence of a traditional novel, as in the image below:

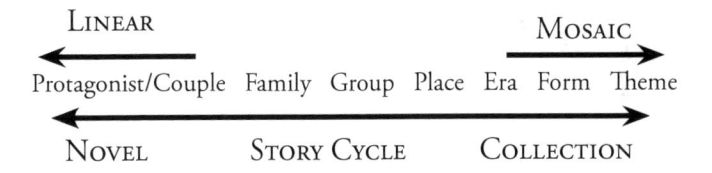

Linear						Mosaic
←						→
Protagonist/Couple	Family	Group	Place	Era	Form	Theme
←						→
Novel		Story Cycle		Collection		

Thematically unified cycles strive for greater unity than we normally get in a traditional collection. The more unified vision is often suggested first in the title or subtitle of the book. There will be no reference to "collected" or "and other stories" following the title, and the title itself often resonates thematically. (Faulkner was reportedly outraged when his publisher initially released *Go Down, Moses* as *Go Down, Moses and Other Stories*.) The thematically unified cycle often focuses on the way the stories inform and counterpoint each other, creating a meta-theme or argument. The title of Antonya Nelson's *Female Trouble* indicates immediately the concerns of her collection. The stories in Updike's *Trust Me* revolve around issues of trust and betrayal. Russell Banks' *Success Stories,* which contains a central-protagonist-based mini-cycle within its larger thematic design, interrogates the American yearning for, and ironies of, success. Andrea Barrett's National Book Award-winning collection, *Ship Fever,* explores the emotional lives of scientists. Although two of my own collections, *Love Songs for the Quarantined* and *Marrying Kind,* rely on a variety of unifying strategies, including macro-designs and some recurring characters, they are primarily thematically linked cycles, as their titles suggest.

Cycles unified by subgenre or form are like thematically unified cycles in that no explicit narrative connection (for example, an overarching plot, a continuing cast of characters, a consistent setting or community) is promised or expected. However, the stories are all *of a kind*, often linked by genre expectations or specific aesthetic premises. In Robert Olen Butler's *Tabloid Dreams,* for instance, each story is narrated by a voice whose origins come directly out of *The National Enquirer,* and Butler treats these characters as if they have complex inner lives. The most famous story from the collection, "Jealous Husband Returns in Form of Parrot," is an apt example, providing us with a husband-turned-parrot as narrator. These characters, though treated literarily, seem to exist in a parallel tabloid universe that is both ordinary and surreal. Butler's experimental collection, *Severance,* is made up of 240-word interior monologues from the consciousness of decapitated victims, both famous (Medusa, John the Baptist, Marie Antoinette, Nicole Brown Simpson) and non-famous (a chicken, a prehistoric man). In *Twice Told Tales,* Daniel Stern uses famous philosophical, psychological, or political texts as the jumping off points for his stories, such as "The Interpretation of Dreams by Sigmund Freud: A Story." Lorrie Moore's first book, *Self-Help,* relies on the suspect form of self-help literature to shape her hilarious and moving stories; titles include "How to Be a Writer" and "The Kids' Guide to Divorce." These cycles all depend, for their full effect, on a high-concept approach.

Historical era-based cycles fall on the story collection end of the continuum. These cycles do tend to embody an epoch or a certain historical moment. F. Scott Fitzgerald's *Tales of the Jazz Age,* Hemingway's *In Our Time,* Adam Braver's *Mr. Lincoln's Wars* (a novel-in-stories), and Kate Walbert's *Our Kind* (with its focus on ten different women who come of age, marry, and bear children in 1950s America) all announce with their titles the sense of an era encapsulated, with only *Mr. Lincoln's Wars* consciously striving for novelistic (or novel-in-stories) coherence.

With *place-based cycles*, we are moving into more familiar long-narrative territory, encroaching on one of the fundamental unities, setting, that we usually expect in novels. *Dubliners,* as I've indicated, is the classic example of a cycle relying on this unifying strategy. Peculiarly, none of the characters in the collection know each other or intersect in any significant way, yet they are all Dubliners, and each story depicts a type of citizen, or a quality of Irish life, that seems to be, for Joyce, representative. James Baldwin's portrait of Harlem in *Going to Meet the Man,* John Updike's *Olinger Stories* (which brings together the stories he had written about his fictional Pennsylvania hometown), Richard Ford's *Rock Springs,* Annie Proulx's *Close Range* (with its investigations of life in Wyoming), and Edward P. Jones' *Lost in the City,* about African Americans in Washington, D.C., are all explicitly or implicitly indebted to Joyce's *Dubliners*.

Community-based cycles are similar to place-based cycles in that they tend to be located in a specific location, but unlike place-based cycles, this type of collection is closer in spirit to the novel, focusing on a culture, community, or group of people whose lives significantly intersect. *The Canterbury Tales* is perhaps the most famous example. There is no central focus on place (the characters are on a pilgrimage) but rather on the community of pilgrims who pass the time by telling each other their stories. *Winesburg, Ohio* is the great modern example; the title suggests that it will focus on a place, but the real focus is on the *inhabitants* in this small town and the way the characters live both isolated *and* intersecting lives. Garrison Keillor's popular Lake Wobegon stories, perhaps the longest-running short story cycle in contemporary literary history, are more benign versions of the Winesburg narrative, shot through with both a stoic Midwestern melancholy and a generous sense of comic mischief. Gloria Naylor's *The Women of Brewster Place* coalesces around the community of African-American women in a housing project, and Robert Olen Butler's Pulitzer Prize-winning *A Good Scent from a Strange Mountain* spotlights sixteen Vietnamese characters who have immigrated to Southern Louisiana after the fall of Saigon.

Family-centered cycles move us into a more recognizably novelistic realm—that of the family saga. The characters are not just connected by geographic location or circumstance, but by blood ties, and the development of the individual characters is always seen through the prism of multigenerational family dynamics. These cycles differ from traditional novels in that the other unities—of narrative focus, of voice—tend to be minimal or absent. Faulkner's *Go Down, Moses* is his most fully realized cycle and really a benchmark for this kind of linked narrative, as are Erdrich's *Love Medicine* and Anne Tyler's *Dinner at the Homesick Restaurant,* a "novel" deeply indebted to Faulkner. Susan Minot's *Monkeys,* Cristina Garcia's *Dreaming in Cuban,* Amy Tan's *The Joy Luck Club,* as well as my first book of linked stories, *Last Call,* are other examples of cycles that make use of the multigenerational family saga as the primary unifying strategy.

Cycles that focus on *a central protagonist or couple* encroach most emphatically on the expectations and formal unities of the novel. These cycles tend to be connected by a loose narrative—most often the story of a relationship, a love affair, the coming of age of a young man or woman (*bildungsroman*), or the development of an artist (*künstlerroman*). One of the distinguishing features of this type of cycle is that it often evolves over the course of the writer's career, with the author returning to favorite characters or alter-egos in a series of books before combining them in a single collection of stories or a loose-knit novel that focuses exclusively on this character or couple. These are examples of what Forrest L. Ingram, an early scholar of the form, called "completed cycles" (as opposed to those "composed" from the beginning or "collected" after the fact). Hemingway's Nick Adams stories and Katherine Anne Porter's Miranda stories fall into this category, as do David Huddle's *Only the Little Bone,* Isabel Huggan's *The Elizabeth Stories,* Fitzgerald's *Basil and Josephine Stories,* Updike's Henry Beck and Maples stories, Justin Cronin's *Mary and O'Neil,* Melissa Pritchard's *Disappearing Ingénue,* Alice Munro's *The Beggar Maid: Stories of Rose and Flo*, Elizabeth Strout's *Olive Kitteridge,* and Charles Baxter's *Saul and Patsy.* Though Tim O'Brien's classic, *The Things They Carried,* relies on multiple unifying strategies, the primary thread holding the book together is the narrative involving the writer-veteran, "Tim," and his efforts to parse out the moral, psychological, and emotional differences between "happening truth" and "story truth."

Beyond these primary unifying strategies, there are less overt but still significant strategies to increase the connections between the stories and intricately establish a sense of patterning and design that can be deeply satisfying for the reader. These strategies include image patterns, rhyming action, counterpointed characterization and plotting, and echo effects. Other kinds of formal patterning involve rotation of point of view, shorter closely linked "suites" of three or four stories, and variety or unity of voice and tone. Story cyclists also frequently employ superficial (though often effective) strategies, such as epigraphs, maps, casts of characters, family trees, section breaks, listed dates of the action and/or narrator names under the title of each story to increase the sense of interconnection and reinforce the impression that the book should not be read for its parts but as an intricately designed whole.

Fundamental Unities, Framework Questions, and Closure

In his 1998 *Writer's Chronicle* article on the form, "The Short Story Novel," scholar and novelist George R. Clay argued for a more intentional approach to writing short story cycles, suggesting that the best "short story novels," as he called them, will have these elements:

> Fundamental unities that distinguish connected from collected stories: place, time, cast, theme, tone, style; a framework question addressed throughout successive chapters and answered by the end, indicating what the novel emerging from these individual stories is about; provisional rather than complete closure for each chapter's "story," creating narrative progression by propelling us, through open-ended interconnections, to the next "story"; a

recognizable protagonist (whether individual, family, or group) to empathize with as we realize what is at stake; and final closure when the framework question is answered and the provisional closures ending previous chapters culminate in a satisfactory overall resolution.

Clay's advice for writing book-length story cycles is, I think, overly prescriptive and discounts the variety of unifying strategies available to fiction writers. He seems to believe that story cycles, as Laura Morgan Green said in a *Poets & Writers* article, "aspire" to be novels, and he wants to nudge them along in their more linear aspirations.

Having said that, I think Clay offers a clear-eyed model of how a cycle can be designed or revised for greater novelistic unity, and he provides useful strategies for writers who wish to increase the level of interdependence of their stories and create the sense of both narrative and emotional progression.

There are no simple methods for creating any work of art. But there are useful questions that may guide or prompt the writer as he or she writes, revises, adds and subtracts material, looking for the most organic and powerful design of a work-in-progress. Below are the questions I find most useful in designing, writing, and revising a short story cycle.

Self-sufficiency and interdependence. Can each story be read and enjoyed without reading the other stories? Can each be published separately? How closely are the stories linked? What is their level of interdependence? Does the arrangement of the stories *matter*—in terms of plot, character development, or theme? Can the stories be easily re-sequenced? If so, does this help or hinder the unity of the cycle?

Linear and/or mosaic design. Is there an overarching narrative or thematic question that is raised at the beginning of the cycle, carried through the book, and resolved at the end? Does the shape of the individual stories or the cycle as a whole depend on linear or mosaic design, or both? Does each story have provisional or complete closure? What are the advantages and/or limitations of each kind of closure?

Character development. Do the protagonists or repeating characters (if present) seem to grow or have a developmental arc as the stories progress? Do the stories chart the characters' moral, artistic, emotional, psychological, or intellectual development? Or do the characters remain relatively static (not necessarily a bad thing), revealed in snapshots over time?

Formal considerations. Are the formal elements of the book (point of view, voice, form, genre, tone, etc.) limited or richly varied? What is the effect of these formal considerations on the unity of the book? Is there rhythmic patterning in terms of images/symbols, point of view, suites of stories, dramatic or thematic counterpoint, rhyming action, or similarity or contrast in form or tone? Is the whole greater than the sum of its parts? If so, how? Is the effect similar to what John Gardner called the "symphonic effect" of the novel, "in that its closing movement echoes and resounds with all that has gone before"?

Masters of the Form

Of course, the best thing a potential short story cyclist can do is study the masters of the form. For my money, Anderson's *Winesburg, Ohio,* Munro's *The Beggar Maid,* O'Brien's *The Things They Carried,* Erdrich's *Love Medicine,* Danticat's *The Dew Breaker,* Egan's *A Visit from the Goon Squad,* and Silber's string of story cycles—*Ideas of Heaven, The Size of the World, Fools,* and *Improvement*—are the most powerful and complex American examples. These books employ the widest array of unifying strategies and have advanced the form in significant ways, both aesthetically and commercially. But I also recommend immersion in the stories, novels, and cycles of writers—such as Faulkner, Joyce Carol Oates, John Updike, and Louise Erdrich—who fully embrace the cyclical imagination and who move effortlessly between the short story, short story cycle, and novel forms, creating large bodies of work that are intricately and intentionally linked.

Faulkner consciously wrote several short story cycles—*Go Down, Moses, The Unvanquished,* and *Knight's Gambit*—but more importantly, his novels operate like cycles, returning to (or recycling) the characters and events of his imagination from book to book, deepening and extending his vision in his great Yoknapatawpha series. Louise Erdrich—in story after story and book after book dealing with her Chippewa and German clans along the Minnesota-North Dakota border—has created a body of work that most closely rivals (some would say exceeds) Faulkner's in terms of scope, ambition, and the depth of its simultaneous self-containment and interconnectedness.

Joyce Carol Oates has said, "My books of stories [are] not assemblages of disparate material but wholes, with unifying strategies of organization." Perhaps more than any other contemporary literary writer, she has written more *kinds* of cycles—from thematically organized collections like *The Wheel of Love* or *Faithless: Tales of Transgression,* to subgenre- or form-based cycles like *Haunted: Tales of the Grotesque* or *The Assignation* (sudden fiction, or "miniatures," as she calls them, clustered around the theme of the title), to collections she transformed, in the writing, into novels that retain their story cycle feel, such as *Marya: A Life.* She has also consciously experimented with ambitious novel cycles, like her four-book postmodernist gothic romances, beginning with *Bellefleur,* which extravagantly deconstruct genre fiction.

The late John Updike was a contemporary master of the cyclical imagination. I'm thinking not only of his astounding quartet of Rabbit Angstrom novels, but also of his three-book series of linked stories about his alter-ego, the Jewish writer with writer's block Henry Beck, or *Too Far to Go: The Maples Stories,* the semi-autobiographical David Kern stories, and his *Olinger Stories,* as well as thematically unified cycles like *Trust Me,* and even a trilogy of novels (*A Month of Sundays, Roger's Version,* and *S.*) that re-imagines and modernizes the central characters and themes of adultery, betrayal, guilt, hypocrisy, and revenge in Hawthorne's *The Scarlet Letter.*

What these masters have accomplished, in both their individual books and in their bodies of work, reveals a path not just for the composition of a single cycle of stories but for a lifelong cultivation of the cyclical imagination.

Under the Influence

WHAT WE TALK ABOUT WHEN WE TALK ABOUT INFLUENCE

As both a writer and teacher, I've been obsessed with the question of influence, both nonliterary and literary. It's informed my fiction, nonfiction, and poetry, not to mention the kinds of undergraduate and graduate courses I've designed, such as Forms of Fiction, Sudden Fiction, Short Story Cycle, Literature of the American Dream, Shakespeare, The American West in Film and Literature, and Family Systems in Film and Literature. I even taught a special topics course for MFA students at Iowa State University entitled the Ecstasy of Influence, in which the students and I explored what we talk about when we talk about literary influence. It was one of my favorite courses—and one that helped me reshape the kinds of questions I now focus on for most of my other creative writing and literature courses.

What *do* we talk about when we talk about literary influence? Some critics and writers believe that the story of a writer's work is the story of that writer's influences—what Harold Bloom famously refers to as the "anxiety of influence." Writers, however, might more profitably embrace Jonathan Lethem's inversion of Bloom's phrase:

"the ecstasy of influence." Imitation is the greatest form of flattery, and some of the most interesting art comes from this explicit impulse to tip one's hat to a master. In music, it's called remixing or sampling. In film, it's called a remake or visual reference. (Think of how many films reference the famous steps sequence from *The Battleship Potemkin*.) In literature, we think of it as intertextuality or homage.

Some kinds of homage are free-form modernizations of texts. Other kinds involve direct engagement with the world of the text itself. James Joyce's *Ulysses*, Charles Frazier's *Cold Mountain*, Margaret Atwood's *The Penelopiad*, and the Coen brothers' *O Brother, Where Art Thou?* all retell Homer's *The Odyssey*. Jane Smiley's *A Thousand Acres* sets *King Lear* in 1970s Iowa. Sena Jeter Naslund's epic *Ahab's Wife* reimagines *Moby-Dick* from the perspective of the mad captain's wife, who is only referenced briefly in Melville's masterpiece. Geraldine Brooks' Pulitzer Prize-winning *March* retells *Little Women* from the father's point of view. Anne Sexton's *Transformations* reinterprets the Brothers Grimm from a feminist perspective.

Sometimes the desire for intertextuality may not be so benign. We don't, as writers, always want to tip our hats. Sometimes we instead want to satirize or pick a fight with a specific literary text, an author, or even a whole genre. *Hamlet* is a deep parody of the popular revenge tragedies of Elizabethan England. *Shamela* is Henry Fielding's satire of his rival Samuel Richardson's sentimental novel,

Pamela. In *Rosencrantz and Guildenstern Are Dead,* Tom Stoppard deconstructs *Hamlet,* telling the tale from the clueless friends' perspective, exposing and emphasizing the histrionic self-indulgence of the Prince of Denmark. In *Possession,* A.S. Byatt deconstructs the Romantics. E. L. Doctorow sends up the historical novel in *Ragtime.* Edward P. Jones reconceives slave narratives in *The Known World. Wild Nights!* is a collection of Joyce Carol Oates' novellas about the last days of such writers as Twain, Dickinson, and Hemingway, written in those writers' styles.

I want to recommend three seminal essays by T. S. Eliot, Toni Morrison, and Jonathan Lethem that served as the intellectual backbone of the course I taught and that helped us more rigorously examine both our literary and nonliterary influences.

In "Tradition and the Individual Talent," T. S. Eliot suggests that "immature poets borrow; mature poets steal." To become a mature literary artist, Eliot argues, you must find a way to "extinguish" or "escape" your personality. The artist is not a personality but a *process*, not a vessel for a personal outpouring of feelings, but an *organism*, or an *instrument*, a *sensibility* designed to create a complex and compelling aesthetic emotion. He recommends that the writer not concentrate on his or her distinctive individuality but rather on his or her place within larger literary and artistic traditions. He poses these kinds of aesthetic questions: What are the traditions in which you must steep yourself—a "self-sacrifice," Eliot would argue—in order to become a mature artist? In what literary history do you want to situate yourself—to keep it alive and/or to alter it by your own art?

In "The Site of Memory," Toni Morrison discusses the way her own understanding of literature and her place within it arose from a "matrix" of slave narratives, personal memory, national history, and the recollections of others. She speaks specifically about the rhetorical strategies and social function of slave narratives, and the difference between what can and cannot be said in those narratives. She writes into the space of the unspoken, the veiled, the mysterious silence of history. She asks writers what matrix they write into, what rhetorical traditions they might subvert, what histories they might rediscover. What is veiled or unspoken or interior that you should examine in your writing? Morrison's primary metaphor for this process is archaeology—what she calls the "site of memory" (her own memory, as well as her family's, her community's, her nation's, her race's), which she attempts to "excavate" through her fiction. Do you conceive of your own work as a kind of cultural and personal archaeology? If so, how? If not, what metaphor best suits your own process—and mission—as a writer?

In his essay (and eventual book), "The Ecstasy of Influence: A Plagiarism"—a title I cribbed for my course—

Jonathan Lethem brilliantly argues that all art is "sourced," whether attributed or not, and that originality in art and writing comes not from our own invention but rather from our influences, which he suggests should be embraced and relished rather than ignored, disguised, or protected in a kind of "usemonopoly." Part of what makes this essay so provocative is that Lethem lets the form of his piece reinforce his argument, using a collage and a free-quoting (without attribution) approach, which he "sources" at the end of the essay.

In these essays, Eliot, Morrison, and Lethem not only demonstrate how to navigate through and steal from your major and minor influences, but also how to own those influences, building upon and adding to already rich traditions and literary communities in which you wish to claim a space. Eliot, Morrison, and Lethem also urge a simultaneously conscious, analytical, creative, and proactive relationship between your writing and reading, and offer methods for exploring that relationship that are both inspiring and liberating.

The Origins of
The Girl from Charnelle

I was born in a small Texas Panhandle town two months after John F. Kennedy was assassinated. Although I lived there for only a year and a half, I spent many holidays and summers in the tiny house where my mother had been raised. Over the years, I learned the details of my mother's traumatic childhood and adolescence in the fifties and early sixties. I imagined what life must have been like for her when her family fractured and she was forced to assume far too much responsibility for her mother, sister, and three brothers. Her childhood home became as haunted for me as I think it may have been for her, and when I began writing fiction, I knew that someday that house and that town would be at the heart of a novel.

I began *The Girl from Charnelle* during one of the periods when I was estranged from my mother. I would not see her for years at a time, as she cycled through many marriages and many other troubled and frequently violent relationships between those marriages. Often I did not know where she lived or even if she was alive. As she drifted in and out of my life, I began to believe that, eventually, the next time she disappeared would be for good. In my first book, *Last Call,* I had written about a character named

Laura Tate, who was based on my mother, but my focus in that book was on her later life, married with children. The novel grew out of my desire to reconnect with that character again—if not with the woman my mother had become, then with the girl she might have been. I wanted to re-imagine her life in the Panhandle town where she was raised and where I was born. I wanted to understand her world in that tiny house. I wound up discovering a family who, though at first resembling my mother's, soon took on a life and drama all its own.

My fictional family had been abandoned by their women—an elopement by an older sister followed less than a year later by the mysterious disappearance of the mother. I focused on sixteen-year-old Laura, left to take care of her father and three brothers. I saw that this family was, like America itself in 1960, on the verge of not only a new era, but changes they could not have foreseen or prepared for. I saw Laura at the town New Year's Eve party, startled by the advances of one of her father's co-workers, and then, surprising even herself, falling into an affair with him. I realized that this affair, and her discovery of her own secret erotic and intellectual life, would force Laura not only to contemplate the complexities of her mother's and sister's earlier decisions, but to struggle with the ways that we all try to leave our families and communities—honorably and with their blessings, if we're lucky, or secretly, in shame, anger, or desperation, if we aren't so fortunate.

Another event in my life deeply influenced *The Girl from Charnelle*. A few years before I began the novel, around the time that my mother and I were initially estranged, my youngest son was born with serious health problems. During the first few months of his life, my wife and I lived daily with the belief that he might die, and that it would be, in some inexplicable and helpless way, our fault. My son is fine now, but the vivid, painful experience of those fragile first months changed me. Since then, I've listened carefully to the stories of families that are devastated, transformed, and sometimes healed by tragedy. About midway through the writing of the novel, I realized that a tragic loss would propel the characters into very different futures than the ones they thought they wanted. And they would be forced, along with the rest of their community, to try to make sense of their grief, guilt, and anger.

During the three years I spent writing this novel, I did not show it to anyone, nor did I talk much about it, not even to my closest friends and most trusted critics. I kept thinking about this line from my favorite Chekhov story, "The Lady with the Pet Dog": "Everything about which he felt sincerely and did not deceive himself, everything that constituted the core of his life, was going on concealed from others." My characters had hidden lives, too. They were mysterious to each other and to me as they clung to their secrets and decided (or were forced) to expose them. In fact, the original title of the book was *The Value of a Secret Life*. When I finished the novel, I felt a great sense of relief and accomplishment, but also deeply sad and vulnerable about releasing these characters to other readers besides myself. These people I'd spent years with were no longer part of my secret imaginative world. But like Laura, I discovered that the value of a secret life lies, in part, in letting that hidden life—and letting the people you love—go.

Writing this novel about a family in crisis made me feel more connected to my own haunted family and, more importantly, reminded me that fiction can profoundly expand both the reader's and the writer's capacity for empathy. The experience of writing *The Girl from Charnelle* rekindled my compassion for those closest to me, no matter whether they stay nearby or drift in and out of my life.

Giving and Taking in McMurtry's West

McMurtry and Me

Larry McMurtry—the author of more than fifty novels, books of nonfiction, and screenplays, primarily about the historical and contemporary American West, including works that have won the Pulitzer Prize and numerous Academy Awards—grew up on a ranch near Wichita Falls, Texas, just down the highway from the Panhandle towns where I spent much of my youth. Before I read his work, I had fallen in love with iconic films based on his novels, *Hud* and *The Last Picture Show,* modern black-and-white classics that juxtaposed romantic images of the historical American West against the harsh, wind-swept loneliness of the contemporary West. I began reading his novels seriously in college, at the urging of my high school English teacher, Dwight Huber, who was an informal scholar of McMurtry's work. I was later surprised to see McMurtry's second novel, *Leaving Cheyenne,* legitimized on the syllabus of a Contemporary American Fiction course I took my second semester in graduate school, a validation of McMurtry's work that eventually inspired me to write my master's thesis on his ambivalent relationship to his Western heritage. My thesis adviser was a young novelist, Richard Russo, who had recently joined the faculty at Southern Illinois University. Russo had studied briefly with McMurtry at the University of Arizona, and had written essay-reviews on some of McMurtry's novels. Russo's novels about small-town American life—such as *Mohawk, Nobody's Fool,* and the Pulitzer Prize-winning *Empire Falls*—are clearly influenced by the sociological seriousness and comic-tragic sensibility of McMurtry's fiction.

At the time of my initial deep dive into McMurtry's work, he was not that well known beyond a relatively small literary circle. McMurtry used to wear a shirt that said "Minor Regional Novelist," a joke about the perception of his status in the literary firmament, as well as a comment on the poor reputation of place-based fiction (beyond New York City) among book reviewers and scholars at the time. *Lonesome Dove,* his epic cattle drive novel, won the Pulitzer Prize in 1986, but the international success of the television series that transformed McMurtry's reputation didn't air until after I had completed my degree. By that time, with Russo's encouragement, I had left my doctoral program in literature, turning away from the theory-heavy and footnote-chasing constrictions of academia, and dreamed of writing my own stories and novels rather than scholarship about the fictions of others.

Both McMurtry and Russo were instrumental in this decision, since they had gone through similar transformations from academics to fiction writers. Russo has remained the most significant influence on me, serving not only as my thesis director for my McMurtry project, but also as the mentor for my MFA thesis, a collection of stories, many of which were published in my first book.

But McMurtry has had a profound and lasting impact on me, especially his first ten books, which I studied carefully—an ambitious body of work that reveals his literary evolution from elegiac chronicler of mid-twentieth-century Texas ranch and small-town life, to comic sociologist of urban life in what he called his "Balzac of the Pecos River" endeavors, to revisionist de-mythologizer of the historical West in *Lonesome Dove*.

These books, written over the first quarter-century of McMurtry's career, were important to me for a number of reasons. First, McMurtry modeled how to turn the people and the places of my world—the Texas Panhandle and Houston, in particular—into literature, something that, as an avid reader and a nascent writer, I had not seen before. It gave me license, though I didn't know it at the time, to tell the stories of my own places and people—Texas and Oklahoma farmers, oil riggers, rodeo riders, restaurant owners, motel clerks, prison guards, waitresses, secretaries, con-men, carpet salesmen, and railroad workers.

McMurtry was raised on a large ranch by his grandparents and great-uncles and great-aunts, who themselves could remember and seemed to embody the ghosts of the nineteenth-century frontier. But McMurtry also was something of an alien in Texas—not just a ranching kid but a bookworm, who gobbled up shelves of literature, both classic and contemporary, an obsession that led him to a side career as an antiquarian book scout and later as an independent bookstore owner. He straddled these two worlds—the rural, working class of Texas and the hyper-literary world of libraries, university English departments, and bookstores—that I myself occupied or yearned to occupy. And he had something to say, as a writer urgently engaged in both celebration and critique of the American West, that also spoke to me.

I continued to follow McMurtry's career, even as I moved on in my own. When I lived in Arizona, where I taught creative writing and literature at a small private liberal arts college, I made a trip to a Phoenix bookstore to hear him read and abashedly gave him a copy of my master's thesis. (He wrote me a gracious postcard in return.) Then one hot summer week in 2011, I made a long-delayed pilgrimage to Archer City, where *The Last Picture Show* had been filmed more than four decades earlier, and where now McMurtry lived, off and on, and where his famous multi-building independent bookstore, Booked Up, was located.

I stayed in the *Terms of Endearment* room at The Lonesome Dove Inn, where McMurtry himself often stayed when in town, rather than at his own ranch a few miles away. I ate and chatted with the proprietor, his friend from Archer City High School days. She told me stories of McMurtry's love-hate relationship with his hometown, and she took my photograph holding his Pulitzer Prize and his Academy Award, which McMurtry let her display in the lobby of the inn.

The marquee of the renovated movie theatre offered well-wishes to McMurtry and his new bride, Norma Faye Kesey (the widow of Ken Kesey), who had recently married in a civil ceremony in Archer City and were now off on their honeymoon. I ate a dilly bar at the Dairy Queen that inspired McMurtry's moving memoir about his quadruple bypass surgery. I rummaged through the disorganized stacks of books in the repurposed municipal buildings of Booked Up and was thrilled to find a used copy of my own novel, *The Girl from Charnelle,* in the stacks devoted to Texas literature. When I left Archer City, the temperature well over a hundred degrees, as it had been throughout my visit, I felt as if I had made good on an overdue promise, like visiting a family homestead that you've only heard stories about—an ancestral home where you seek a palpable connection to your past.

Focused primarily on McMurtry's *All My Friends Are Going to Be Strangers,* the essay that follows is a case study in both personal and literary influence. McMurtry wrote the book quickly, over a few months, riding on the fumes of the thousand-page novel, *Moving On,* that had burdened him for nearly a decade and that he had just published. *All My Friends* reads to me now as a form of exorcism—McMurtry grappling with the literary and cinematic history he has written into and against throughout his career. For all its darkly satiric humor, the book is also a provocative, and at times harrowing, study of a writer at a vocational crossroads, questioning the psychological costs of being a novelist, using his life and the lives around him to feed his art. As its enigmatic title suggests, it's about those for whom the world has been turned inside out, with friends, family, and lovers transforming into strangers and one's beloved home into an alien landscape.

Giving and Taking in the American West

McMurtry's underappreciated fifth novel, *All My Friends Are Going to Be Strangers* (1972), is a key text in the study of his fiction—not just for its artistic value but also for the way it illuminates his complicated relationship to his work and to the thematic obsessions that have haunted him throughout his career. It is a fascinating portrait of an artist on the verge of a nervous breakdown, a postmodern novel that deconstructs itself, ending with the embattled writer-narrator literally in a death-match with a manuscript that he feels has betrayed him, that has robbed him of an opportunity for an ordinary life. In addition to marking a turning point in McMurtry's increasingly critical attitude toward his frontier heritage and his own vocation as a writer, the novel is also important for fiction writers to study, especially writers like myself, a generation or two younger than McMurtry, who write about the contemporary American West and find themselves haunted by many of the same thematic and narrative concerns that McMurtry, who casts a long shadow over the literature of Texas and the West, has examined in his fiction and nonfiction.

In his early and illuminating collection of essays, *In a Narrow Grave: Essays on Texas,* McMurtry emphasized the ambivalence he had always felt about his home state and indicated explicitly his decision to leave the ranch behind and explore the "unredeemed dreams ... in the suburb and along the mythical Pecos": "The reader ... will have noticed a certain inconsistency in my treatment of Texas past and present. A contradiction of attractions, one might call it. I am critical of the past, yet apparently attracted to it; and though I am even more critical of the present I am also quite clearly attracted to it." McMurtry's first two novels, *Horseman, Pass By* and *Leaving Cheyenne*, were moving elegies for the dying cowboy and rancher traditions.

His next four books, however, led him progressively to the belief that the myths of the West were not only dying or dead but insidious. These doubts culminated in *All My Friends Are Going to be Strangers,* which inverted the elegiac tropes of his earlier work. Whereas *In a Narrow Grave* and the sprawling *Moving On* showed him to be increasingly critical of the Western myth, particularly as it manifests itself in urban environments, the more compressed *All My Friends* suggests that McMurtry was ready to repudiate the myth altogether.

The novel charts the emotional breakdown of a young Texas novelist, Danny Deck, and at every turn in the plot, Danny becomes more alienated not only from his friends, family, and lovers, but also from the values and traditions of his frontier heritage. In fact, as Raymond L. Neinstein pointed out in an afterword that accompanied the 1981 edition published by the University of New Mexico Press, the novel "questions everything McMurtry had assumed, and that we as readers of regional literature had also assumed, about place, about writing, and about their tenuous connection." The novel de-romanticizes and de-mythicizes everything McMurtry evoked in his earlier fiction. In "The Frontier Myth and Southwestern Literature," Larry Goodwyn suggested that McMurtry was the young novelist "most embattled in terms of the frontier heritage." By "frontier heritage" Goodwyn meant treating the history of the American West as "the unexamined legend—the propagandist Anglo-Saxon folk myth," which is pastoral, masculine, and racist.

The initial critical reception of this novel was decidedly ambivalent. Some early reviewers were outraged, disappointed, and confused by what seemed a bitter attack on McMurtry's home state. One angry Texas reader noted that the Texas of McMurtry's mind was "about five coon-ass miles southwest of reality." In "Larry McMurtry—A Writer in Transition," Alan F. Crooks found himself "yearning" for the "old McMurtry." And other critics were skeptical as well. In her article, "Journeying as a Metaphor for Cultural Loss in the Novels of Larry McMurtry," Janis P. Stout suggested that *All My Friends* is "a chronicle of tedium," "littered" with "patterns of emotion-laden encounters" and "undeveloped characters." And Kerry Ahearn claimed, in "More D'Urban: The Texas Novels of Larry McMurtry," that McMurtry "looks for eccentric detail related to social, sexual, or Western myths" and "he seems intent upon exploiting the contemporary Western experience."

Regardless of the mixed initial critical opinion, *All My Friends* certainly marked a crucial turning point in the development of McMurtry's relationship to this "unexamined legend" and served as a significant preamble to his increasingly resonant exploration of this legend in his acclaimed *Lonesome Dove* tetralogy, in his other novels which traffic more explicitly in irony and parody, such as *Anything for Billy* and *Buffalo Girls,* as well as the later Berrybender cycle and screenplays, such as his Academy Award-winning adaptation of Annie Proulx's celebrated story, "Brokeback Mountain."

In *Walter Benjamin at the Dairy Queen*—McMurtry's revealing and eloquently sober meditation on his life as a writer, reader, book scout, and bypass-surgery survivor, and on his emotional relationship to the frontier traditions of his father and grandfather—he discusses his attempts to de-mythologize the frontier: "My experience with *Lonesome Dove* and its various sequels and prequels convinced me that the core of the Western myth … is unassailable. I thought of *Lonesome Dove* as demythicizing, but instead it became a kind of American Arthuriad, overflowing the bounds of genre in many curious ways." He goes on to say, "Readers don't want to know and can't be made to see how difficult and destructive life in the Old West really was. Lies about the West are more important to them than truths."

More recent studies—especially Mark Busby's astute *Larry McMurtry and the West: An Ambivalent Relationship* and John M. Reilly's *Larry McMurtry: A Critical Companion*—acknowledge the significance of *All My Friends* in the early development of McMurtry's increasingly critical relationship to his frontier heritage. But few critics overall have spent much energy analyzing the relationship between the novel's thematic concerns and its artistic design and narrative strategy.

All My Friends Are Going to Be Strangers is a dark and probing satire about an artist's connection to his work. It also represents McMurtry's most sustained examination of the way postmodern culture distorts the traditions and values of the frontier, and the way those very values promote emotional isolation in the contemporary West.

What most interests me is the way McMurtry's ambivalence toward his frontier heritage is expressed in this novel in terms of what one of his characters calls "giving and taking," a thematic dichotomy which appears with greater and greater degrees of complexity in each of his novels. In McMurtry's second book, *Leaving Cheyenne*, this dichotomy is formally introduced, as Mr. Fry, the old philosophic rancher, explains to Molly Taylor, the heroine of the novel, the difference between givers and takers. "Some have to take and some have to give and a very few can do both," he says. "I was always just a taker, but I was damn particular about what I took, and that's important." He goes on to tell her, "You could take a million dollars, but instead you'll give out twice that much to sorry bastards that don't deserve it." Later, Molly tries to assess what she knows and doesn't know about herself and about life, and Mr. Fry's statement sticks in her mind: "I knew an awful lot of things about myself. What I liked to eat and smell and do. And I knew some bigger things than that—about giving and taking."

While my focus here is on *All My Friends,* I believe the central thematic struggle in each of McMurtry's novels and screenplays involves his characters attempting to balance these altruistic and self-serving approaches to life. McMurtry shows us how the giving and taking pattern works on both the social and personal levels, with a sensitivity to the way the cultural context, especially the historical frontier and its alternately heroic and corrosive psychological legacy, impinges on his characters' emotional lives.

In *All My Friends*, Danny Deck comes to believe that the more he gives to his writing—that is, the more he gives to the fantasy relationships he creates on paper—the less he is capable of giving himself to real relationships. This discovery alters everything he had previously believed about who he is, his role as a writer, and his connection to the values and the myths of Texas. Danny's situation is complicated by the unstable social context in which he finds himself. Like most of McMurtry's young urban characters, Danny is "swirling" in the confusion of city life. Unlike the ranch (which in McMurtry's previous novels provides tradition, coherence, and moral stability), the city offers only, as Patsy Carpenter in *Moving On* senses, "foggy, mushy ambiguities." Danny discovers that his relationships to his cultural heritage and to other people are rapidly shifting.

Divorced from the ranching traditions—or any kind of cultural tradition—McMurtry's characters continually find themselves frustrated and isolated, and their frustration often erupts in displaced violence. In *Moving On*, Patsy remarks to herself that the transient life of the urban West "breeds some kind of violence." Similarly, in *All My Friends*, the constant rush of the city gives rise to a disturbingly unhealthy attitude toward life. Mr. Fitzpatrick, Danny's landlord, for instance, cannot stand the thought of Danny and Danny's wife, Sally, making love. His garage is next to Danny's apartment, and when he returns home, usually drunk, he listens intently for any evidence of sex that might trigger his anger. At one point he rams his car door against Danny's wall, screaming, "No fucking! No fucking!" as Danny and Sally run nakedly about trying to catch flying pots and pans.

The novel abounds with characters like Mr. Fitzpatrick, who lead dislocated and hostile lives, or, who like Danny himself, lead lives that "veer crazily one way and then another, like a car being driven by W. C. Fields." McMurtry's depiction of urban life is, in fact, often bitterly satiric, and many of his best readers have tended to focus on the author's critique of contemporary social values. For instance, Janis P. Stout, one of the more perceptive scholars of McMurtry's work, claims in the essay I referenced earlier:

> None of the characters [in *Moving On* and *All My Friends*] has any sense of a usable past, and none is purposefully directed toward the future. They inhabit the burgeoning cities of Texas with no apparent means of orienting themselves and nothing to engage them but endless, unsatisfying motion—as the title *Moving On* well indicates. The problem, of course, is that they are not moving on toward anything.

Indeed, *All My Friends* depicts the contemporary West as a place that breeds rootlessness, violence, and sexual and emotional isolation.

Cannibalism and Thievery

The effect of being cut off from one's cultural heritage is a kind of starvation. Images in *All My Friends* associated with hunger and with eating form a major thematic pattern. In his early novels, images related to food play an integral role in differentiating givers from takers. McMurtry's female givers—Halmea in *Horseman, Pass By,* Molly in *Leaving Cheyenne,* Genevieve and Ruth in *The Last Picture Show*—are all linked somewhat conventionally to a warm kitchen. They nourish others both literally and figuratively. In *Leaving Cheyenne,* Gid does not just desire Molly; he is "starving" for her. The scene in which Mr. Fry explains the difference between giving and taking to Molly ends with the following: "Molly, if I was just ten years younger I'd take your whole two million myself. The rest of the pack could go hungry. Gid would probably be the first one to starve."

In *All My Friends*, overeating and malnourishment become even more significant. Danny is both literally and figuratively starving. Throughout, we see him constantly gorging himself. In an early episode, he even shoots a squirrel in a neighbor's yard, cooks it, and eats it (this after having just finished off half a chicken). Moreover, in almost every chapter, he stuffs himself with junk food: "Nibbling took my mind off my troubles so I nibbled all day." Fig Newtons, Dr Peppers, Mounds candy bars, Tootsie Pops, Butter Rum Life Savers, Fritos, jalapeno peppers, and bean dip form the "staples" of his diet. In McMurtry's first two novels, although the characters were often unhappy, they did at least eat well. Similarly, they were to a large extent nourished by their cultural heritage, especially the ranching traditions. Danny, however, is cut off from those traditions, his most viable link to them, at best, an unhealthy one: "Trashy food was my heritage." This point is made most clear when Danny returns home to visit his Uncle Laredo's Hacienda of the Bitter Waters, a place where "everything ... seemed to be starving."

Significantly, Danny receives his only good meals from Emma Horton (who would later become the protagonist of the bestselling novel and Academy Award-winning film, *Terms of Endearment*), who performs a role similar to that of Halmea, Molly, Genevieve and Ruth in the earlier novels. Like them, Emma is most at ease in her kitchen, where she can "do for others." For Danny, her kitchen comes to represent home, a place where he is nourished and accepted. By the end of the novel, it symbolizes everything that is worthwhile in life and, by extension, everything he feels he has been denied: "The door to the ordinary places was the door that I had missed.... There would never be an Emma's kitchen for me," he mournfully says. But the warmth of Emma's kitchen is the exception rather than the rule in the novel.

Whereas in McMurtry's earlier works eating was a positive act, associated primarily with giving, in this novel, images associated with eating become surprisingly and often surrealistically connected with taking: in fact, cannibalism becomes a dominant metaphor in the new West.

In the second chapter the theme is formally introduced as Danny indicates that he is collecting material for a book he means to write, to be called *Cannibalism in Texas*. His primary subject for this book is his next door neighbor, Jenny Salomea, "a man eater": "It was generally agreed that Mrs. Salomea"—her name overtly alluding to the biblical figure who requested John the Baptist's head on a platter—"was eating [her husband] alive, one joint at a time." At a party held by a Rice University professor, Danny is introduced to a trio of lesbians; trapped between them, he felt like he "was in the middle of a school of piranha fish," and he "tried to look humble and unappetizing." When Danny visits his Uncle Laredo at the Hacienda of the Bitter Waters, he notes, as he looks at the "motley collection of edible animals" surrounding him, that "all of them looked as desperate as the cowboys—on Uncle L's ranch it was an open question as to who would eat whom." And later in San Francisco, after his wife "represses him out of existence," even Danny becomes "a hungry vapor that happened to drift into the room."

The emphasis on taking as a common practice of urban life is also emphasized by the number of characters in the novel who are literally or figuratively thieves. McMurtry's contemporary West is not only cannibalistic. It's a place where "robbery breeds robbery." The robbery motif is present in many of McMurtry's novels and integrally linked, I believe, to McMurtry's thematic conception of taking. Hud's thefts are perhaps the most obvious. In *Leaving Cheyenne,* Gid and Johnny half-seriously josh about "stealing" Molly away from one another, and Eddie does exactly that to them both. In *The Last Picture Show*, Sonny "steals" Coach Popper's wife and Duane's girl, Jacy. The most extended episode in McMurtry's seventh novel, *Somebody's Darling*, involves Jill Peel's theft of the film she directed from the Hollywood company that financed it. *Cadillac Jack* has a major spy and robbery motif running through it. And in *Lonesome Dove,* Call and Gus steal from "Mexican thieves" the horses and cattle that they later drive to Montana.

All My Friends opens with Godwin Lloyd-Jons, the rich English sociologist, wandering about his Austin home accusing everybody, particularly Danny, of "stealing" Sally away from him. Sally's thuggish boyfriend, Chip, is arrested for stealing motorcycles. Geoffrey, Godwin's lover, brings a gang to Godwin's house and tries to extort three hundred dollars from him. In Hollywood, Leon O'Reilly, the film producer, takes Danny's novel and totally reworks it, so much so that Danny feels like his novel has been stolen from him. In San Francisco, when Danny explains his marital problems to a group of bohemian writers, who call themselves "The New Americans," they tell him, "You should bring your wife here…. Somebody would take her away from you."

The New Americans are led by a Texas writer named Teddy Blue, an ironic commentary on McMurtry's part. Teddy Blue and The New Americans are in one sense based on Ken Kesey-type Merry Pranksters. (McMurtry and Kesey were in the Stegner writing program together at Stanford, and McMurtry's *In a Narrow Grave* is dedicated to "Ken Kesey, the last wagon-master.") Yet Teddy Blue (Abbott) was a nineteenth-century writer who chronicled the Charles Goodnight cattle drives in *We Pointed Them North,* which McMurtry argues is "by any standard, a superb memoir; and far away the best book on the trail-drivers." The New Americans are characterized here as strange hippies who lack a clear sense of direction and is probably meant as McMurtry's inside joke for those aware of American frontier literature. This characterization is also clearly related to the more obvious parodies of Uncle Laredo and the Texas Rangers (who later in the novel are characterized as violent hippie bashers).

One chapter ends with a visit to Uncle Laredo's wife's house. As they leave, Laredo enlists Danny in an effort to steal fifty of her goats because she wasn't "gettin' away" with a previous "goddam robbery." Perhaps the most persistent thief in the novel is Sally, Danny's wife: "I couldn't make her my friend. She doesn't have feelings. She'll take anything," says one character whose husband Sally "stole." As the novel progresses, Sally becomes more and more associated with theft, culminating ultimately in her acquisition of Danny's "seed": "My one practical function in Sally's life had been to get her pregnant.... All she had needed of me was my seed. I gave it and that was that. In all other respects she was self-sufficient. She didn't even say thank you for the seed."

Throughout his career, McMurtry has always been a mournful, if ironic, moral anthropologist. In this milieu of surreal cannibalism, of constant robbery, it is no wonder that ethical values are distorted. Early in the novel, Danny suggests that he has no "moral coordination," an odd term, but one which aptly captures both his feeling of moral loss and the consequences of that loss—a sense of emotional and ethical imbalance.

The word "balance" becomes a buzzword in McMurtry's next novel, *Terms of Endearment*. As in this novel, it suggests not physical but emotional and psychological balance: "In the stillness of the night [Emma] felt her own lack of balance," and later Aurora tells her, "You're not a balanced person, Emma … you've always had this self-destructiveness." A lack of psychological and moral balance plagues most of McMurtry's urban characters.

Danny's condition is indicative of his culture as well, for throughout the novel characters either wistfully or bitterly comment on the waning values of postmodern life. A Russian woman at one point tells Danny, "There are no standards here." That fact is made astonishingly concrete by the antics of Antonio, Uncle Laredo's crazed ranch hand, who copulates with everything on the ranch—goats, camels, gas tanks, post holes—and who, Danny later finds out, "was always fucking people, stealing cars, and drinking whiskey." His fellow ranch hands ultimately feel they must leave the ranch because they "cannot live with this Antonio no more. He has got no morality!"

Many critics have found Antonio particularly offensive and unrelated to the narrative except as an additional grotesque parody of the Old West. Yet his role in the novel is actually more thematically integral. Raymond L. Neinstein, in his afterword to *All My Friends*, suggests one compelling aesthetic reason for Antonio's inclusion in the novel: "The antics of Antonio ... parody the metaphor, also strongly present in much of McMurtry's early fiction, of the land as an erotic force, wild, free, fertile, and giving. We can see that metaphor at work in *Leaving Cheyenne*, where Molly Taylor both represents and also literally is ... the 'lay of the land.'" But there are other artistic reasons beyond this one. Antonio's antics—"drinking," "fucking," "stealing"—ironically mirror Danny's. Near the end of the book, Danny goes on a long drinking binge. Sally and her parents label him as a "sex maniac." And Danny, too, is a thief. Antonio has "no morality," and Danny has "no moral coordination." Danny's fate seems inevitable. The ranch hands tell him that Antonio will probably have his head beaten in by "some Texas Rangers." Similarly, Danny is brutally beaten by Texas Rangers near the end of the novel. McMurtry is making a direct connection between Danny and Antonio, which serves as both foreshadowing and commentary not only on the contemporary West, but also on Danny's particular plight.

The givers in the novel, by contrast, are characters who in some way maintain a vital link to their cultural tradition or who maintain their private standards, despite the contemporary erosion of values. The family of Mexicans who take in the naked Godwin during the flash flood, the Mexican ranch hands who cannot live with Antonio's immorality, the old Mexican couple hitchhiking their way to central Texas to see a dying relative, and even Juanita, the prostitute who maintains a "dignity about herself," are each characterized as givers. Similarly, Wu, the old Chinese writer who befriends Danny in San Francisco, wants to give the young writer the benefit of his experience. Emma and Jill emerge as the primary givers in the narrative, and even cannibalistic Jenny Salomea becomes a giver by the end. Ultimately, Danny discovers that the traditional standard bearers, the Anglo males—the Texas Rangers, the Teddy Blues, the Uncle Laredoes—no longer serve as positive role models:

> I had stopped feeling sorry for myself. No more feeling sorry for myself. Why should I? None of my models in life felt sorry for themselves. Not Emma, not Jenny, not Jill. Not Juanita. It was odd that all my models in life were women, but no

odder than a lot of things. Wu was a sort of model.

He didn't feel sorry for himself.

Psychologically and ethically, Danny finds himself caught between and connected to both the givers and takers. Throughout, Danny yearns to be important to somebody else, to make others happy. On many levels, he succeeds. Although Danny has good cause, he refuses to abandon either Godwin after the flood or Sally after she "represses him." He gives two sets of hitchhikers rides. He gives the old Mexican couple his car near the end of the novel. He gives his first novel to Wu, the epilogue and prologue to Emma, and his second novel "to the sea." And for all his sexual escapades, Danny is actually very conventional. He wants desperately to love and be loved: "I wanted [Jill] to love me more than ever, not just for me but so she could feel normal." He is a good man, as Jill, Emma, Jenny, the Uncle Laredo's ranch hands, Godwin, and Juanita all at one time or another tell him.

Yet, whether he wants to be or not, Danny is also a taker. In the first chapter, Godwin accused Danny of being a "fucking little thief." (All writers, by trade, are thieves, according to Godwin, appropriating not just the narratives but the lives of others.) As the novel progresses, Danny seems more and more guilty of the accusation. He steals a library book. He steals an octopus. He steals Jill's baby bed story. And almost every woman with whom he has sex or falls in love—Sally, Renatta, Jill, Jenny, and Emma—is either married to or involved with someone else.

The significance of Danny's thievery does not become clear, however, until he visits the Hacienda of the Bitter Waters. There, he doesn't find the West he liked to believe in, nor the types of heroic characters he remembered from the legends, nor even the types of characters he had been writing about. Uncle Laredo is not the nurturing old custodian of the frontier heritage that one had come to expect in McMurtry's fiction up to this point. He is instead a "mean old sonofabitch," who spends his days stabbing the earth, poking holes in it, because he "wanted to get in as many licks at it as he could before he died." His ranch is a place that encourages marital violence (Martha tries to shoot Uncle Laredo), sexual distortion, and thievery—a place that fosters "no sense of sociability." Although Danny leaves the ranch, vowing never to return or to write about it, he, consciously or unconsciously, carries with him, like an infectious disease, the negative values of the nineteenth-century Westerner.

Up to this point, Danny's taking has been harmlessly comic. Once he leaves the Hacienda of the Bitter Waters, however, this aspect of his character takes a violent turn for the worse. Isolated in his twentieth-century horse ("El Chevy"), Danny, like a parody of a nineteenth-century desperado, "rush[es] on toward the battle." Over the course of the next few chapters, he nearly kills a man, verbally assaults his in-laws, betrays his best friend, is responsible for another friend's beating and arrest, and literally drowns his own novel. By the end, he becomes, in his own words, a "criminal." The stealing, the brutality, the individualism, the romanticism, the isolation that are, for better or worse, inextricably a part of the Western American heritage only prepare Danny to be a misfit in the contemporary West. He has learned that he cannot be simply a giver. In order to survive, in order to avoid leading "a dog's life," he believes he must take Godwin's and Jenny's advice and learn to "call a bitch a bitch." But such a lesson comes at a steep emotional price for Danny, for he does not relish the idea of being a thief—"I was not out to rob [Juanita] of her reserve"—nor does he "like being the hurter."

Swirling

Unable to make any sort of positive connections with others, with himself, or with his culture, Danny finds himself in an emotional and moral "swirl."

Early in *All My Friends*, Danny tells us that this condition comes upon him frequently, particularly when he is intoxicated: "When I'm drunk, things swirl. Once in a while they stop and I notice something before the next swirl begins." But the feeling is more than just a physical sensation. The word itself accrues symbolic meaning as the novel progresses, foreshadowing the ending and serving not only as McMurtry's commentary on Danny's plight, but also, by extension, the plight of a new generation in the contemporary West.

At almost every important juncture in the novel, the word recurs. When he receives news that his novel will be published, Danny feels himself propelled into a dreamlike state: "Things were swirling." In the flash flood scene, Danny notes the "water swirling around my legs." The story Danny steals from Jill involves an "interlocking swirl of lovers and boyfriends and mistresses, ex-mistresses, wives, ex-wives." Right before throwing Geoffrey over the balcony, Danny indicates that "the Austin night swirled around us, warm and familiar." In the last chapter, as Danny, drunk and exhausted, drowns his novel in the Rio Grande, the word occurs nearly a dozen times. In the final scene, as he floats down the river, Danny notes Peter Paul on the bank calling him back: "If my friends came and asked him why I had left he wouldn't know, he had never stood in the river, I don't think he swirled as I was swirling, he didn't seem to yearn to flow, he didn't want to be undertaken."

The constant repetition of "swirl" in relation to romantic expectation and inebriation, sex and violence, and, finally, with passivity and self-destruction creates a provocative and disturbing pattern. Divorced from the positive aspects of his cultural heritage, separated from those he cares for and yearns to give himself to, sensing that he has unwittingly become a taker—a "hungry vapor," a thief, and a "hurter"—Danny feels he has no alternative but to "flow," to "swirl," to exile himself from "the country of the normal," from the world of Emma's warm kitchen, to "the country of the strange." Earlier in the novel, during the flash flood, Godwin strips and plunges into the flood waters, explaining that he must submit himself to "the destructive element." The scene is a telling one, for Danny, too, must ultimately submit himself to the same element.

In *Leaving Cheyenne*, Mr. Fry had advised Gid to "fight the hell out of life." But in the new urban West, overwhelmed by the "foggy, mushy" ambiguities, Danny, McMurtry seems to suggest, is doomed to "swirl."

In light of such a harsh critique of the contemporary West, McMurtry's vision appears almost nihilistic, and the bitterness of his satire seems like a sharp break from his previous work. Yet the novel operates on another, more redemptive level. In a 1972 interview conducted shortly after *All My Friends* was published (which I discovered in a Twayne Series monograph on McMurtry by Charles D. Peavy), McMurtry suggested that his novels are not simply disguised autobiographies or fictionalized social commentaries: "[W]hile the books are partly about me, partly about a place, partly about our time, they are, I hope, chiefly about the characters who live them." Although Danny is to some extent representative of an age—representative of a culture dislodged from its traditions—he is also a complex, idiosyncratic character, not to be completely abstracted from his own context or historical moment, from his own special desires, needs, and motivations. Although Danny winds up in a "swirl," to him that swirl is not necessarily life-negating. In fact, McMurtry probes to what extent that "swirl"—with all its sexual, cultural, and emotional ambiguities—is positive and even life-affirming.

Most critics have suggested the opposite view. Kerry Ahearn, in the previously cited "More D'Urban," claims that the novel—indeed McMurtry's whole early urban trilogy—signals what he calls his "decline to success," a regression to a popular type of art that does little more than "parade the freaks before us." And in "Journeying as Metaphor for Cultural Change," Janis P. Stout argues that, because McMurtry emphasizes the fragmentation of modern life, his novels "lack cohesive form" and finally become "imitative to a radical and destructive degree." Concerning the ending of *All My Friends*, Stout suggests that

> Though some of [Danny's] meditations ... seem to indicate return and renewal after the immersion in the river, the predominant quality is renunciation of his life.... He seeks dissolution in rivers and the great sea of the unreachable past.... The sense of finality, hence of death, is accented by the preceding

> abandonment of his car, which itself seems near death.... The implication is that by giving up his means of journeying, Danny is giving up living.

Ahearn, by relegating Danny to the level of "freak," misses much of the complexity of the novel. And Stout, by overemphasizing the negative aspect of Danny's final act, excludes the ambiguities—conscious on McMurtry's part—of that act.

In contrast, Raymond L. Neinstein and Barbara Granzow, two of the most sympathetic early readers of the novel, acknowledge the complexity of Danny's motives. In "The Western Writer: A Study of Larry McMurtry's *All My Friends Are Going to Be Strangers*," Granzow argues that Danny, by the end, is caught between cultures, between the frontier legacy left to him and the consequences of that legacy: cultural and psychological isolation. "Danny's fate," she suggests, "seems to be borders, in-between places where his old friends have become strangers and any new 'possible friends' are also strangers." Danny's final plight down the river is meant to be a sadly heroic one—even though the notion of heroism has been greatly diminished in the new frontier.

In the interview referenced above, McMurtry offers some indication of how complex Danny's motives are, but he suggests that the character's motives are not the author's.

He claims that the only autobiographical part of *All My Friends* is Danny's questioning whether writing is healthy. According to McMurtry, writing can be self-destructive and a "tricky thing to manage throughout a lifetime":

> It is true that the better you write the worse you live. The more of yourself you take out of real relationships and project into fantasy relationships the more the real relationships suffer. The popular theory is that writing grows out of a neurosis, and is a cure for neurosis. This is nonsense. It may grow out of neurosis, but it doesn't cure it; if anything, it drives it deeper and makes it nearer to being a psychosis.... I do not think that writing, or any art, pursued seriously, is necessarily a health producing activity. Writing involves a kind of gambling with the subconscious and the destruction of self-defenses.

McMurtry forces Danny to explore this relationship between writing and life: "He has some sense at the end of the book that it is hopeless," McMurtry says about his antihero, "that either he won't be much of a writer, or that the better he writes, somehow, the more it's going to alienate him." In other words, Danny begins to believe that there is not enough of himself to go around. If he gives to his writing, he will inevitably abdicate any hope for ordinary happiness.

In the Destructive Element Immerse

In *All My Friends*, this question of whether artistic endeavors are destructive is also posed by Godwin and Jill. Godwin claims, as I've said, that writers are thieves, that they unscrupulously take from life and put little back into it. And on several occasions, he warns Danny to abandon his vocation: "As soon as you're divorced [from Sally], give up writing. Do those two things at once and you've at least a chance for happiness.... Wait much longer and it may be too late. There are no writers in heaven, you know. They don't even know how to enjoy the bloody earth." And Jill, an artist herself, provides experiential evidence to support Godwin's claims. Although not a writer, she knows firsthand how her artistic work has alienated her from others, cut her off from normal and healthy relationships with her child and with others she has loved: "I don't want to love anybody. I don't want to repress anybody out of existence, either. I'm not a woman anymore, I'm just an artist. All I can do is draw. It'll happen to you if you don't get a girl.... You'll wake up someday and you'll just be a writer. I'm not worth it. Nobody's worth it. You'd be better off staying a man." Jill is the one who encourages Danny to give his novel "to the sea" as a sacrifice. And later, sensing that Danny has already become an artist like herself, she writes to him, "I don't want you to be cursed like me, but I'm afraid you may be already."

In an early comic episode, one of the women at the party, like the witches in *Macbeth,* places a curse on Danny: "Your keys will no longer fit in locks. No door you really wish to enter will open for you again.... Soon a pane of glass will drop between you and your wife.... The pane of glass will enclose you like a cylinder, separating you from all women. You will want many women, but nothing will ever shatter the pane of glass." Although Danny thinks little of the scene (and does not refer to it again), each aspect of the curse is fulfilled. Danny ultimately comes to believe that the source of his troubles, of his isolation, is language itself. He feels, as Raymond L. Neinstein suggests, "trapped in a maze of words, suffocating, lost, cut off from what he had taken to be his place, his family, friends, and lovers." In the first chapter, Godwin tells Danny that all writers "ought to be imprisoned," and by novel's end, Danny feels imprisoned in a "house of fiction," a "city of words." "I hadn't engaged with anyone," he says. "I was very separate. My words got across to people, but it was all verbal. At a deeper level, some level of needs and responses to needs, I was separate from everybody."

His disillusionment culminates in one of the final scenes of the book, as Danny questions his own motives for writing: "I looked at my pages under the flashlight. They looked odd. Words. Black marks on paper. They didn't have eyes, or bodies. They weren't people.... Jill had a face. Emma had a face. My words didn't…. I didn't know what I was doing, spending so much time with paper."

Seen in this light, Danny's final actions are not life-negating. On the contrary, given the dialectic that has occurred in the text, his actions (in his mind at least) affirm his realization about the impotency of language and the dangers of being an artist. Danny is attempting to undo the curse. Throughout the novel, writing has become associated with taking: with cannibalism, with stealing, and ultimately with cruelty. In short, with a denial of life. "I remembered Jill's anger when she said I had been doing what I really wanted to do when I wrote…. It was an awful thought…. I would rather have her with me than to write all the books I would ever write." In his attempts to drown his own creation, he acts sensibly, responsibly, even heroically. Jill had told him to give his novel to the sea, and indeed he has, along with himself. He finally follows Godwin's lead and immerses himself in "the destructive element."

The phrase "the destructive element" comes from Conrad's *Lord Jim*, and it is important to note Conrad's passage here, for it offers a special insight into Danny's motives for his final act:

> A man that is born falls into a dream like a man who falls into the sea. If he tries to climb out into the air as inexperienced people endeavor to do, he drowns…. No! I tell you! The way is to the destructive element submit yourself, and with the

exertions of your hands and feet in the water make the deep, deep sea keep you up. So if you ask me—how to be? ... I will tell you! ... In the destructive element immerse.

Given the image patterns established in the novel, the destructive element, the sea itself (Danny loves to read all narratives associated with oceans, rivers, and seas) becomes a positive symbol of life. He drowns his novel, McMurtry suggests, so that he does not have to drown himself.

Danny wants "to flow, to be undertaken," to be buoyed up by life. In giving himself to the sea, in effect becoming one of "the ordinary little people who for some reason or another decided to journey up the Amazon or explore the Andes," Danny yearns no longer to be an artist with all that vocation has come to imply, but to be "simply a man." His reappearance in McMurtry's *Texasville,* and later as the narrator of *Some Can Whistle*, suggests that he indeed survived his ordeal.

The Westering Experience

In many ways, this novel represented a temporary departure for McMurtry. His next four novels would deal less and less with the contemporary frontier or with the Texas experience. Danny's ordeal evidently had a great effect on its author. After McMurtry finished the novel, he stopped writing for two years. And when he returned to fiction with *Terms of Endearment*, he came to conclusions similar to Danny's, as he notes here in this quote from his *Atlantic Monthly* essay, "The Texas Moon, and Elsewhere": Novelists "exploit a given region, suck what thematic riches they can from it, and then, if they are able, move on to whatever regions promise yet more riches." Those words "suck" and "exploit" have direct connections to the thievery and cannibalism motifs in this novel, as well as to the oilman imagery of earlier novels. In his afterword, Neinstein makes a good case for *All My Friends* being a regionalist novelist's "farewell to regionalism."

But there is a clear connection between Danny's predicament and the predicament of characters in his previous and subsequent fiction. McMurtry has increasingly concentrated on the emotional consequences of vocation or any kind of obsessive work. Homer, Mr. Fry, and Gid—the major figures in his first two novels—are characters who have to some degree profited from their giving to the land, from their devotion to ranching as a way of life. But emotionally, their lives have become cramped and mean, "miserable," as Mr. Fry suggests. Vernon in *Terms of Endearment* and Woodrow Call in the *Lonesome Dove* tetralogy find themselves in the same situation—stoically compelled to work their lives away. Given this preoccupation with the emotional and spiritual constrictions of frontier life, it's no surprise that McMurtry would be so enamored of

Proulx's, "Brokeback Mountain." (He has said that "Brokeback Mountain" was one of only two stories written by another writer that he wished he'd written, the other one being an unidentified Grace Paley tale.) The more that McMurtry's characters devote themselves to their work—the more they identify themselves first as ranchers, oilmen, Texas Rangers, or writers and artists, and only secondarily as humans—then the more they alienate themselves from restorative sources of life.

In *Walter Benjamin at the Dairy Queen,* McMurtry writes,

> What rodeos, movies, Western art, and pulp fiction all miss is the overwhelming loneliness of the westering experience.... Many Westerners were alone so much that loneliness was just in them, to a degree that finally made domestic and social relations difficult, if not secondary. The old joke that cowboys get along better with horses than they do with women is not a joke, it's a tragedy. The kinds of demands that the unfenced, unplowed, unwatered West made on human attention and human energy seemed to me to solitarize rather than socialize. Somehow the outlaw came to stand for this solitary Westerner—the man who has no ties because he kills. More common was the man

who had no ties because he would rather work and keep working.

This isolation points to the most dominant and complex feature of the giving/taking pattern in McMurtry's fiction—its connection to the frontier and American work ethic, a Puritan mindset that praises work and to a large extent condemns the pursuit of physical, cultural, and emotional pleasures. McMurtry continually calls into question this work ethic, which promises a fruitful life from toiling, from eking out an existence in an often brutal country, whether it be the arid plains of American West or the blankness of the white page.

What has this labor, this devotion to place and work, cost emotionally? How has this devotion depleted any kind of fruitful relationship with others? Does our fidelity to work—or in Danny's case, to a vocation that both metaphorically and literally imprisons and drowns him—make us more giving, more responsive human beings? Or does it turn us, unwittingly, into symbolic thieves and cannibals? Or worse, into Uncle Laredoes, doomed to live on a Hacienda of the Bitter Waters, striving only to get in "the last lick" before we die?

These are the difficult questions McMurtry poses in *All My Friends Are Going to Be Strangers*. They are the questions that will increasingly obsess him in his later and more famous work, most notably in *Lonesome Dove*. And they are questions, poignantly illuminated in this provocative and underrated gem, that seem more relevant than ever to contemporary writers, Western (like myself) or otherwise.

On the Road: The Do-It-Yourself Book Tour

Talking to a group of fifty sixth-graders at a prep school in Mobile, Alabama during homecoming week was not my idea of big-time book promotion. I was three weeks into a ten-week book tour for my collection of linked stories, *Last Call*, which won the Prairie Schooner Book Prize in Fiction and was published by the University of Nebraska Press in 2004. My wife and I, along with our four kids, were staying at my wife's uncle's house, and I had agreed to give a short reading and talk for her young cousin's class. When I heard it was homecoming week—the floats were being constructed in the courtyard below me—I winced. And yet, when I read a short passage about a girl falling off a horse (one of the few G-rated passages in my book), the crowded room of eleven-year-olds was absolutely rapt. They were not yet old enough to have forgotten the great pleasure of listening to a story. I asked for questions, fully expecting to carry the Q&A session myself. To my surprise, thirty hands shot up.

"Can you tell us about the publishing process?" asked a serious young girl, her notebook in hand. "And then I have a follow-up question."

"Do you and your kids fight? Because me and my mom fight all the time," another boy confessed. I later learned from the teachers that he was the headmaster's son.

When I asked the kids if they wanted me to read another short passage, they cheered. I later told my wife, "Every writer deserves this kind of audience."

That event in Mobile was just one of many surprises of the ten-thousand-mile, ten-state, sixty-event tour that I had cobbled together. Reading at a barbecue dinner at the small Tennessee university where my father-in-law teaches, addressing an audience in Amarillo that included the high school English teacher, Dwight Huber, who inspired me to write, visiting Flannery O'Connor's peacock farm, Andalusia, during a gig in Milledgeville, Georgia, speaking to inmates at a medium-security prison in Childress, Texas, as well as watching my four kids strong-arm bookstore patrons into buying my book—these were among the most memorable events of what I called, depending on my level of whimsy, "The Great *Last Call* Book Tour" or "The Great Futon Tour."

It will come as no surprise to any creative writer that trade publishers no longer routinely send their authors on extensive book tours. That privilege is usually reserved for bestselling celebrity authors; the rest of us are lucky to have a marketing department splurge for print ads or postcard, e-mail, and social media campaigns. University and independent presses have even fewer resources to offer their authors, and many writers are left to their own devices or encouraged to spend their small advances to hire private publicists.

Of course, even writers who are sent on reading tours sometimes complain about them, and for good reason. The embarrassing turnouts at bookstores, the hectic traveling schedule, the unexpected expenses, the time away from family and normal writing routines—it's enough to make you wonder whether it's all worth it. Yet a book tour is still one of the great mythical perks of literary success, and it remains the best way to build an audience, develop promotional skills, and more importantly, share work directly with readers—no small matter given how long most of us write in silence and obscurity.

When my collection won the Prairie Schooner Book Prize, I was determined to make the most of the situation. Everyone told me that the success of my collection depended on my ability and willingness to promote it and that there was a very small window of opportunity for its success. I was prepared to make an investment of money, time, and energy to give *Last Call* the best chance possible. I negotiated an early sabbatical from Prescott College, where I taught creative writing and literature, spent several months planning a tour, got in touch with my inner salesman, and then hit the road with my entire family and several boxes of books. My goals were clear: sell books, build an audience, develop contacts, and pave the way for my next book. But I also wanted this tour to be *fun*—not a lonely experience but something I could share with family, friends, students, mentors, and colleagues.

Because I knew I would be on a half-salary leave from my faculty position—the one that allowed me to provide for my four children—I had to begin saving far in advance, and then I had to count pennies throughout the tour. I determined that the cost of lodging could potentially derail the entire endeavor, so I plotted my trip not through major literary hubs but to places where we could visit and stay with family, friends, colleagues, mentors, and friends-of-friends. I planned an extended stay in Nashville in late October to coincide with the due date for my sister-in-law's baby. I arranged trips to off-the-beaten-literary-track cities like Las Cruces, Mobile, Milledgeville, and Childress because we wanted to see friends and relatives—and let them rustle up audiences for me. We researched opportunities and diversions for the kids as well—stops at the Alamo, the Texas State Capital, Helen Keller's birthplace, Sea World, and space and science centers in various cities. (The "Grossology" exhibit at the Witte Museum in San Antonio was a particular favorite.) And I planned a two-week stay in the Texas Panhandle; not only is the area one of the major settings in my book, but I also have family there who would happily feed and house us.

I don't think I've ever worked harder in my life than I did during the ten weeks of the tour. A typical day for me would include loading up my minivan (not an easy thing to do with a cargo of six travelers, luggage, and boxes of books), driving for several hours, visiting two or three classes, shaping a reading for a particular event, eating lunch or having dinner with students, teachers, and event coordinators, driving to a Kinko's at midnight to print handouts, setting up events two weeks down the road, and then sleeping for a few hours before starting all over again. There was, in fact, a nearly sleepless seventy-two hours when I had reading gigs in Memphis, Nashville, Louisville, and Austin. Before I embarked on the tour, I naively believed that I would have time to write new fiction while I was on the road, but I soon gave up that romantic notion and realized that, for these two months, I was a salesman, hocking my wares out of the back of my appropriately named Honda Odyssey.

Before every event, I thought of my friend Bret Lott's great essay, "Toward Humility." In it, he describes being flown on a Learjet to what everyone expected would be a huge, standing-room-only signing for his novel, *Jewel*, a recent Oprah Book Club pick. He arrived, however, to find only a few of his former students and a woman with a dog in a baby stroller. The woman bought a book and asked him to inscribe it to the dog.

I kept my expectations low. I never expected to sell a book, and so I was always delighted if I sold five books or fifty.

Setting up events for the tour was a challenge. I didn't want to preclude a good gig even though it would not pay. However, I gave higher priority to those events that offered at least some remuneration—a small fee, a place to stay, or access to a larger audience of potential readers. Because I'd been a professor at a small liberal arts college for many years and also co-coordinated a regional reading series in Arizona, I felt most comfortable arranging events at colleges and universities. These gigs often involved a reading and a Q&A session, a short craft talk, or guest visits to creative writing or literature courses. Series coordinators typically generated publicity through student or local newspaper articles, posters, and website notices.

The events often attracted good-sized, attentive audiences because faculty members required their classes to attend my readings. I had the opportunity to answer a variety of questions, ranging from the typical prying autobiographical inquiries ("Did you really drive your car into a lake?") to complex questions about form, technique, and process. I sold a reasonable number of books, and because academic institutions actually *believe* that such readings are culturally enriching, I was often given a modest honorarium to help defray travel costs. I found that smaller colleges and universities were more receptive to emerging writers like me visiting campus, especially if the book or author had a regional connection. As a tie-in to my visit to West Texas, for example, a professor at my undergraduate alma mater adopted *Last Call* for an advanced online course. Students read my work, attended my reading, and wrote essays and creative work inspired by my stories; for seven days, we exchanged emails on a university-sponsored bulletin board—a great thrill for a writer and teacher—and one of the highlights of the tour.

Whenever possible, I worked in the classroom with students. I knew from experience that one of the best ways to develop an audience was to offer something beyond my own writing, to become part of an extended community of writers and readers. So I spent the majority of my time on tour not just reading but teaching—with many visits to grade school, high school, undergraduate, and graduate creative writing and literature classes, and a ten-day residency at Spalding University's MFA Program in Writing, which turned out to be a community I've remained affiliated with—the best gift of all. My ability and willingness to teach ultimately accounted for the overall financial success, as well as many of the most memorable events, of the book tour. Some of my favorite gigs—almost all of which I stumbled upon by accident—took place in public and private middle schools and high schools. I expected these events to be difficult and draining, but the students were generally funny and focused. They didn't often buy books, but months later I continued to get charming e-mails from them. I planned to be writing for a long time, so I figured I was already building a future audience.

While I read or did signings at numerous independent and chain bookstores, I discovered that most cities also have alternative venues. Among the best of these are literary centers that sponsor readings as well as special workshops that writers can teach. For example, Gemini Ink, the prominent literary center in San Antonio, invited me to give a reading as part of their monthly author series and to teach a four-day workshop on sudden fiction for community members. Libraries, too, were great resources and particularly receptive to readings and workshops. The librarian in Dumas, the small Texas Panhandle town where I was born, set up a full day of events at the local high school and then arranged a nice evening reading and reception at the community college extension center. I was also fortunate enough to read at the Texas Book Festival as a featured author. I queried the festival coordinator, stressing my regional connections, and was invited to participate.

Of course, it was crucial to find out what an event coordinator wanted—a reading, a Q&A, an informal talk, a craft discussion—and how much time I would have. By the end of the tour, I had about ten different kinds of presentations I could give—readings of complete stories or excerpts, a discussion of the stories behind the stories, a tour through the book, or more formal analyses of craft, using short excerpts as illustrations. I've been to enough readings over the years to know that they can be deadly—actually working against a writer, making an audience *not* want to buy the book. So I thought of the reading as a form of performance: an introduction to the book and to me. Above all, I tried to remember that the audience was there to hear a good story, not to watch the author fidget self-consciously or read in a monotone. I wanted each event to provide something the audience member couldn't get from simply buying and reading my book.

I wish I had done more media events on my tour, but I was able to do several newspaper interviews, a couple of radio interviews, and even one television spot (*Good Morning, Amarillo*), all of which I arranged by contacting newspapers and radio and television stations directly. The public relations director at the college where I taught wrote a press release, tailored it to the individual cities where I traveled, and sent the release to the editors of local and regional newspapers. Because I didn't have a private publicist, this support was invaluable, and the publicity benefited the college, too.

While my publisher devoted most of its modest budget to print ads, a postcard campaign, and generating reviews (all great things), they also co-sponsored, along with the journal *Prairie Schooner,* a nice event at the University of Nebraska for which they paid my expenses. And the press was wonderful about providing me with extra books to use for promotional activities. Since practically every event coordinator or media contact needed a copy of the book, this additional support was crucial. When I asked for more postcards and publicity materials, they printed them for me. Perhaps most importantly, my publisher let me sell my books. While my preference at every stage of the process was to have a bookstore purchase books and do the selling for me, that was not always feasible, especially since my itinerary often changed. When I scheduled a new event, I needed quick access to books to sell. Every few weeks, I would have my publisher ship a few more boxes to one of my future destinations.

All of this work ultimately paid off. By the time I arrived in Nebraska, six weeks into the book tour but a mere week and a half after the official publication date of the book, I had already sold more than half of my print run. The modest honorariums, income from selling books, payment for various teaching gigs, the generosity of family and friends who housed and fed us, and the extra tax deductions transformed the tour from a potentially bankrupting endeavor into a financially successful enterprise.

More importantly, I'd achieved the intangible goals I'd set for myself of building an audience and sharing the book with a few thousand new readers. When I first heard that *Last Call* had won the prize, I was at Blue Mountain Center, an artist colony in the Adirondacks. A fellow resident there, Hannah Tinti, a short story writer and novelist and one of the founding editors of *One Story*, who had worked for many years in the publishing industry, offered sage advice. She encouraged me to be aggressive with publicity and to remember that the opportunity to promote a book is a privilege, not a burden.

The day after the final event of The Great *Last Call* Book Tour, my agent called to tell me that she'd just sold my second book, a novel entitled *The Girl from Charnelle*, to William Morrow Publishers. I couldn't have scripted it any better.

By late November, after two months of touring—traveling a geographical loop that began in the Southwest, dipped down through Houston and into the Gulf Coast bayou country, and extended as far east as Georgia and as far north as the plains of Kansas and Nebraska—I finally arrived in the Texas Panhandle. A few days before Thanksgiving, my uncle drove me from Amarillo down to Childress where my grandmother had been a reporter and editor for the local newspaper for about thirty years and where my mother had recently moved. I had asked them to set up any events they wanted me to do in Childress. There was, of course, a big spread in my grandmother's paper. And my mother had arranged three events: five classes at the local high school, a visit with the residents of an assisted-living center, and a talk at the medium-security prison. I said to my wife: "Great, three captive audiences, none of them able to buy any books."

By this point in the tour, I was exhausted and ready for it to be over. This would be the final series of events before heading home to Arizona for a return celebration and reading. Of the three events in Childress, I was most nervous about the prison visit, not only because it was a prison with every kind of offender, from white collar to violent, but also because my mother, grandmother, and uncle would all be in attendance. Although I had been teaching since I was twenty and, by then, giving readings for more than a decade, no one in my family had ever seen me do either.

As we made our way through each level of security, my bladder grew weaker and weaker. There was a long wait when a security check didn't clear, resulting in the threat of a lockdown. We passed a small room, and I could see about ten inmates through the thick glass window. I asked if that was the group attending my talk. The education coordinator calmly said, "No. That's the anger management class."

Finally, we were led into the prison's library. Tables had been moved and chairs set up to create a small theatre. My mother, uncle, and grandmother sat in a row of chairs to the side, like a jury. I sat on a stool at the front of the room as sixty-five inmates wearing white jumpsuits entered— some very young, some middle-aged, some old and barely able to walk. Suddenly, I felt incredibly relaxed. These were just men, men who had made mistakes, probably terrible mistakes they grieved over—one of the central themes of my book. I told them about myself, and then I read a story based on my father about a con-man who tries to buy Costa Rica and whose plane, like my own father's, crashed in the jungle. When I read a passage about the mother in the story, who makes her living selling bras and lingerie, the men simultaneously swiveled their heads toward my mother, who, at almost sixty, was still a looker.

I told them about my family and the way they had inspired many of these stories, and then I read excerpts from a piece about an oil rigger suffering from heat stroke on an offshore rig, who longs to reunite with his estranged wife. And then we talked and laughed about stories as gifts—gifts you give yourself and others—and about imagination and about the self-imposed exile of writers, the necessary silence that was sometimes not unlike prison.

Though I didn't sell a book and couldn't even leave postcards (which were considered contraband), that was the best event of the entire journey. Without quite knowing how to articulate it, this was what I had wanted when I dreamed of a book tour and had worked so hard to prepare for it: to be in a room with people—myself and my family included—who needed stories to make sense of, and to help transform, their lives.

Sena Jeter Naslund and the Ecstasy of Influence

I joined the faculty of Spalding University's low-residency MFA in Writing Program in the fall of 2004, early in the program's history. My first book had won a prize and was about to be published, and as I detailed in my previous essay, I planned to embark, with my wife and children, on a 10,000-mile, ten-week, ten-state, do-it-yourself book tour—"The Great Futon Tour," I called it, because my family and I relied for our lodging on gracious relatives, former mentors, friends, and friends of friends along the way. I had planned to come through Louisville on this tour and had sent an email to Sena Jeter Naslund, the founding director of Spalding's MFA program and the author of many books of fiction, including the bestselling and acclaimed novels, *Ahab's Wife* and *Four Spirits*. I didn't know Naslund personally, though I was friends with one of her former colleagues at the low-residency program at Vermont College, where Naslund taught for almost two decades before launching the Spalding program. I had received my MFA from Warren Wilson College, another low-residency program—in fact, for many years, one of only two programs in the country, along with the one at Vermont College, both programs offshoots of Goddard

College, which had in the 1970s created this model of low-residency education for creative writing.

In my email, I asked merely to come through Louisville, perhaps give a reading and interview Naslund for some research I was doing on arts administration. It turned out that the program needed a last-minute replacement for a faculty member in fiction for the November residency. Naslund asked me to overnight my book to her. A few days later, she called, told me she enjoyed *Last Call*, then said, "Now let's talk turkey." I couldn't believe my good fortune, as it had long been my dream to teach in a low-residency program, having experienced first-hand, as a student, how transformational this kind of education could be.

The Spalding program is particularly special, a bona fide gift community of the kind I described earlier in the book—borne of friendship and mutual commitment to an ideal method of graduate education and training in creative writing that stands apart from the prevailing culture of many MFA programs, which can often be hotbeds of rivalry, artistic jealousy, and competitive hostility, places where familiarity breeds contempt. Naslund had worked as a professor at many colleges and universities—Vermont College, the University of Louisville (where she served as the director of the creative writing program and distinguished professor and writer-in-residence), and the University of Montana, among others. She wanted to pioneer a different philosophy and practice of graduate education in creative writing, based on principles of egalitarianism and respect, but more importantly a combination of encouragement and rigor—a place where "every individual talent is nurtured" and where faculty members and students are treated with similar respect as fellow artists. She didn't want to just pay lip service to these principles, but to have the program embody them.

One of the great privileges of my professional life has been to be part of this community—to mentor students who come to the program with their own rich, complex histories and aspirations, to work alongside colleagues whose careers and lives I admire, and to not only experience Louisville and the intense residencies, which are simultaneously exhausting and exhilarating, but also other parts of the world during the program's moveable feast of international residencies (London, Buenos Aires, Barcelona, Rome, etc.), an innovative residency model that Naslund pioneered because, at a faculty meeting, a faculty member jokingly asked if we could have the next residency in Paris. "Why not?" she said, and a year later a small group of faculty members and students were talking craft in the shadow of the Eiffel Tower.

One of the best perks of this job was the opportunity to work for and with Naslund, who retired in 2017—listening to her masterful craft and plenary lectures and her quietly thrilling readings, watching the way she led by example, with a rare combination of disciplined intellectual rigor, encouragement, compassion, and joy. I loved strolling around Stratford-upon-Avon, Shakespeare's hometown, with Naslund and debating with her and my playwriting colleague, Charlie Schulman, the merits of *The Merchant of Venice*. I also loved learning to tango in Argentina with her and other faculty members and students, and dancing, at a hacienda on the Pampas one glorious evening, while steaks smothered in chimichurri sauce awaited the completion of our revels.

Though Naslund was not my mentor, she has been one of my most important influences—as a colleague, as an academic administrator, as a model for how to successfully marry life as an educator with life as an artist, as a person who is fiercely independent and tough-minded and yet an unflagging champion and defender of friendship, good will, and enriching communities for writers and artists.

At the residencies, I have enjoyed and learned a great deal from her about not only the art of fiction, but have benefited even more from hearing her speak about her own journey as a writer—her struggles to find her voice and to earn recognition for her work, her national and international triumphs, how she's juggled her commitments as a teacher, mentor, administrator, parent, and friend with her passion and increasingly ambitious mission as a novelist.

She has modeled with particular grace how to carve out a meaningful life in letters—how to survive the lean years, how to reinvent yourself as an artist when you have exhausted your original store of material, how to remain true to core principles while staying open to unforeseen possibilities, how to be creatively vital beyond youth and middle age, how to invigorate yourself as a writer by helping other writers, whatever their ages, find their voices and refine their visions and midwife their manuscripts into the literary world. My colleagues, students, and I have been fortunate to have had, at Spalding, this writer of international renown whose life and career we can continue to study for inspiration.

In November of 2017, at age seventy-five, Naslund officially retired, in part to commemorate the retirement age of her own mother, who was also a teacher, and in part to devote more time to the new historical novel she had begun—her most ambitious project to date. I was fortunate to deliver the keynote lecture for Spalding's retirement celebration of Naslund, called *SenaFest*, honoring her career as a writer, teacher, mentor, and leader of the program. This essay is adapted from that lecture and is designed to offer, for those who haven't yet delved into her fiction or who want to rediscover her books, some entry points that have been valuable to me as a writer.

In particular, I examine two major sources of influence and energy in Naslund's fiction—literary tradition (as in her ekphrastic deconstructions of Sherlock Holmes mysteries, *Moby-Dick,* the Book of Genesis, and *Portrait of an Artist as a Young Man*) and history (as in her panoramic visions of nineteenth-century America, Birmingham in the 1960s, and France during the Marie Antoinette era). Naslund's ambitious, deeply inhabited novels offer us, as fellow writers, essential strategies for exploring the subject, structure, style, and significance of our own writing projects.

Naslund and the Ecstasy of Influence

As I explored in an earlier essay, some critics and writers believe that the story of a writer's work is the story of that writer's influences—what the critic Harold Bloom famously refers to as the "anxiety of influence"—a kind of half-conscious Freudian war that writers have with their literary fathers and mothers. Naslund's approach to influence, both in her writing and teaching, was and is more benign and intentional. She actively promotes homage, intertextuality, and informed creative conversations with those who have influenced us. At the opening night event of every residency, she would repeat her credo to the students, faculty, and staff assembled: "Our competition is not in this room. It's in the library." During the residencies, Naslund insisted upon full-program outings to art museums, plays, concerts, Churchill Downs, and other Louisville art spots as a way to discover new sources of inspiration for our writing and celebrate the interconnectedness of all the arts. But it wasn't enough that we took these trips. She would routinely engage the faculty and students in ekphrastic exercises—writing inspired by other art—based on these excursions, generative exercises that refreshed our writing and offered new aesthetic directions.

In his essay and eventual book, "The Ecstasy of Influence," Jonathan Lethem argues that all art is indebted, whether attributed or not, and originality in art and writing does not necessarily derive from our own invention but rather from our influences, which he suggests should be embraced, relished, and celebrated rather than ignored, disguised, or relegated to a hostile closet of semi-conscious, quasi-homicidal anxieties. Lethem urges a more conscious, analytical, and proactive relationship between your writing and reading, and a method of going about it that is both inspiring and liberating.

I believe that this crucial notion—using your influences openly, consciously, and ecstatically—is at the heart of Naslund's fiction and defines her ambition and major accomplishments as a writer. She has carved out her own place in the literary landscape in large part by being in direct conversation with—and sometimes open argument with—classic texts, authors, genres, literary movements, and traditions.

We see Naslund tapping this rich vein of energy and inspiration in a number of books. In *Sherlock in Love,* she imagines her way into Arthur Conan Doyle's famous series of Sherlock Holmes' mysteries. Naslund said she embarked on this project playfully, as a kind of lark, but also to teach herself how to plot, a skill that she felt was underdeveloped, especially for the grand epics she hoped to embark upon after completing this novel.

Her eighth book, *Adam and Eve,* is set in the near future, and as the title suggests, is in direct conversation, even argument with, the Book of Genesis. Her most recent book, her ninth, *The Fountain of St. James Court; or, Portrait of the Artist as an Old Woman,* contrasts two older female artists, one historical, one contemporary—the famous French portrait painter and companion of Marie Antoinette, Élisabeth Vigée-LeBrun, who lived into her eighties, and a Louisville novelist, Kathryn, who shares some of the trappings of Naslund's own life (Kathryn, among other things, lives in Naslund's house and shares Naslund's middle name) and who has just completed the novel we are reading about Élisabeth in alternating chapters.

As the subtitle of this novel suggests, Naslund is in conversation with and critical of James Joyce's *Portrait of an Artist as a Young Man,* arguing not so much against

Joyce's portrait of the autobiographical Stephen Dedalus, but against the idea that the only artists worth writing about are young, male, and on the cusp of productivity, rather than portraits of a more diverse range of artists—especially more mature and successful female artists, still grappling beyond sixty with their art and their lives. The novel, in part, rejects Joyce's subject and champions instead Joyce's contemporary (and for Naslund, the greater artist), Virginia Woolf. *The Fountain of St. James Court* openly examines and draws upon the modernist sensibility—as well as embraces Woolf's subtle argument in all her books that every day is worth recording, worth remembering, worth celebrating and savoring—a foundational belief that ordinary life and "moments of being" are just as worthy a subject for fiction as the dramatic event, both of which are artfully juxtaposed in this novel.

Ahab's Wife and Ekphrastic Deconstruction

Ahab's Wife, Naslund's fifth novel and her breakthrough book, reimagines Herman Melville's *Moby-Dick* from the perspective of the mad captain's wife, Una Spenser, a character who occupies only a few lines in Melville's narrative. Naslund grants epic Melvillian space to Una's journey, while Melville's characters on the *Pequod,* including Ahab, play only secondary or minor roles.

I have a few things to say about the subject, structure, style, and significance—crucial coordinates in Naslund's own analysis of literature—of this novel. But first, I'd like to briefly address the origin story of *Ahab's Wife*, which I find moving and inspiring. Naslund has shared parts of it at the Spalding residencies, as well as in interviews. *Sherlock in Love* had just been published and had received a glowing review on NPR. Buoyed by the encouragement and the validation, she felt confident, giddy, and particularly receptive to the muse, which appeared in the form of this sentence—"Captain Ahab was neither my first husband nor my last."—and an image of a woman on a widow's walk. She had been reading and listening to an audio book of *Moby-Dick,* with her young daughter, glorying in the language, the quality of thought, and the narrative expansiveness of Ishmael's tale. She was struck by the way her daughter was captivated by Ahab's speeches and seemed able to quote parts of them from memory. Yet Naslund felt disappointed and saddened that there was no equivalent epic quest in American literature that featured a heroine of similar brilliance, courage, complexity, and eloquence as Ahab and Ishmael. She wanted to write into that gap, to rectify that deficiency.

There were other forces acting upon Naslund as well, but these seem to have been the primary ones. So she embarked on her own epic, multi-year journey in her fifties, without an agent or publisher, writing her thousand-page narrative about Una Spenser's quest for a home, for a place in the world—a novel full of wondrous and terrifying events, lighthouse idylls and sea-faring cannibalism, multiple romances, madness, encounters and friendships with some of the great intellectuals of the time (Margaret Fuller, the astronomer Maria Mitchell, Frederick Douglass, a creepy black-veiled Hawthorne, and many others)—written not so much as a deconstruction or refutation of Melville's masterpiece but as a penetrating conversation with Melville, a "companion book" to Ishmael's book, as Una says at the end of *Ahab's Wife*.

I love this story of its origins, and you can feel the joy, the audacity, the sheer chutzpah, on every page. Naslund had published several books before and had received modest acclaim. But suddenly, seemingly out of nowhere, here is a novelist discovering and energized by her subject, by this artistic premise big enough to wrap her mind, heart, and ripened talent around. It is a giddy reading experience. I once asked Naslund, in a public forum at St. Lawrence University, where I was teaching at the time and where Naslund visited as a guest writer, how she found the stamina and the courage to write such a big, daunting book that so openly challenged one of the great, if not the greatest, American novels. She said, calmly and self-assuredly, with a wide grin, "You don't send a minnow after a whale."

What a wonderful *ars poetica*, what a bold mission statement. "Whatever you do, or dream you can," Goethe once said, "begin it: boldness has genius, power, and magic in it." This book—and the books that followed *Ahab's Wife,* especially *Four Spirits* and *Abundance*—have an unmistakable boldness of spirit matched by a technical virtuosity that a reader, having read her previous four books, would have been hard pressed to predict. There is a sudden, radical leaping forth, an artistic courage emerging from her newfound confidence in her talent, and just flat-out exuberance.

I believe that exuberance arises primarily from the ambition of the endeavor—both the subject and significance of the book. "I really did feel that there was a vacancy in the concept of nineteenth-century American women," Naslund has said. "So I wrote [*Ahab's Wife*] partly for political reasons, partly for my daughter. I wanted her to be able to quote a character who wasn't Ahab, but whose language was resonant."

Una herself says at one point early in her book, "And if one wrote for American men a modern epic, a quest, and it ended in death and destruction, should such a tale not have its redemptive features? Was it not possible instead for a human life to end in a sense of wholeness, of harmony with the universe? And how might a woman live such a life?" This book is that affirmation, an answer and a symbiotic companion to the tragic vision of Melville.

What fascinates me about Naslund's approach to structure in *Ahab's Wife* is her confession that before this novel, she really did not have much skill or talent with plot. As I mentioned, she had taught herself specific plotting skills with *Sherlock in Love,* but nothing that would suggest an ability to tackle a project of this magnitude and that would require a great deal of narrative propulsion to command the reader's attention through a thousand manuscript pages.

Her technical solution to this issue of structure seems to be four-fold.

First, she was fortunate in the gift she received from the muse; the essential structure of the book was nestled in that opening sentence: "Captain Ahab was neither my first husband nor my last." The reader embarking upon the journey has at least three romances to look forward to, as well as the suspense of discovering who the husbands other than Ahab will be and what kinds of relationships they will offer Una. There's a built-in comparative design, and encoded in that structure is a deep meditation on marriage—not only between Una and her husbands, but between Una and other prospective grooms (there are several). But there's the added delight of the marriage between Una and Ishmael as narrators of, as Una says at the end, "the same book." And above and beyond that, there is the literary marriage of Naslund and Melville as novelists and fellow artists. When asked if she was intimidated by Melville and *Moby-Dick,* Naslund has said repeatedly, both in lectures and in interviews, "I wasn't intimidated by Melville. I was inspired!" Her novel is ultimately, I believe, a celebration of marriage, in the largest conception of that word, as a relationship between equals, founded upon admiration and inspiration.

Secondly, Naslund had the idiosyncratic structure of *Moby-Dick* itself—the epic voyages, the tragedies, the philosophical ruminations, the secondary and minor characters, the time-frame, the settings—to work within, much like a jazz virtuoso riffs around a familiar melody, both honoring and transforming it. *Ahab's Wife,* though epic in size, is made up of short, titled Melvillian chapters, which provide their own kind of energy and temporary self-containment, helping us as readers (and perhaps her as a writer) navigate our way through the narrative, giving us hand-holds and natural opportunities to pause and contemplate. Part of the pleasure of reading this book, if you're familiar with *Moby-Dick,* is studying how she operates within Melville's interstices, filling in the gaps, repurposing his characters, finding ingenious ways of making the world she's imagined fit within Ishmael's narrative while simultaneously encompassing the more narrowly defined tragedy, expanding the worlds of both books.

Third, Naslund discovered in the writing of this novel what she calls her "grappling-hook" method of plotting—often leaping ahead to big scenes, as if throwing a grappling hook toward a solid piece of dramatic real estate. When these big scenes would appear in her imagination, she'd leap forward and write them, and then go back to where she left off and "pull herself," as the author, "up the narrative line." A wonderful metaphor and a very practical strategy if you are, as she was, attempting a project more enormous in scope than you've ever tried before.

And finally, Naslund allowed herself and Una to be free from the tyranny of conventional linear plotting; she released herself from the straitjacket of chronological time. "While my quill was poised in the air, not writing, I formed my first principle as a storyteller," Una says late in the novel:

> I will not be governed by time. Time does not march; it swirls and leaps. Time is a dancer, not a soldier. And the second: adherence to fact is slavery. Think how Shakespeare distorted, compressed, rearranged historical events in his history plays. Such license would be mine, if I wrote. When I pieced a quilt, I did not place the pieces in

chronological order, the oldest in the upper-left-hand corner! A pleasing design, color, beauty—could those be my business?

And indeed the novel swirls and loops, moves back and forth and back again, according to memory and instinct, in the way Virginia Woolf, Naslund's idol, operates to be sure, but also in the way that Melville himself operates in *Moby-Dick*, letting us follow the retrospective voice in search of itself, in search of an ordering principle beyond any fixed chronological notions of narration.

And this voice—the retrospective voice—is also the primary feature of style in *Ahab's Wife*. The most significant triumph of the novel is Una, her searching, ruminating, despairing, joyous, straightforward, slightly antique but strangely intimate voice. It's not the plot that keeps us turning the pages, or at least not what keeps me turning the pages (though there's plenty of delicious plot), but rather Una, who serves as the *sound* of the book. This is a great feat of method acting, of historical ventriloquism, of channeling—a *tour de force* of point of view as the embodiment of style, point of view not as simply a literary device or technique but as the substance and sensibility of the book.

There's not enough space in this essay to do justice to that voice, but I want to point toward an emblematic passage where Una (like Ishmael in *Moby-Dick)* reaches beyond the narrative, through time, to talk directly to the reader, to bring the reader more deeply into the story, to make the reader a co-creator and even a conspirator:

> But do you know me? Una? You have shipped long with me in the boat that is this book. Let me assure you and tell you that I know you, even something of your pain and joy, for you are much like me. The contract of writing and reading requires that we know each other. Did you know that I try on your mask from time to time? I come as a reader, too, reading over what I have just written. If I am your shipbuilder and captain, from time to time I am also your comrade. Feel me now, standing beside you, just behind your shoulder.

Una's voice *is* her character. Her voice *is* style. Naslund's brilliant decision in this novel is her crucial choice about point of view—and then having the artistic stamina to maintain such a performative act over such a long narrative. That's chutzpah, that's audacity, that is the real boldness that has genius, power, and magic in it, and makes this book eerie and uncanny, as if Naslund is a sorceress, conjuring spirits from the deep and then becoming those spirits, while at the same time giving order, shape, and artistic coherence to the work as a whole. It's a grand achievement—this ability to create not just characters but artists who are themselves capable of authoring the books they inhabit.

Naslund would do this again, with equal if not greater audacity, in *Abundance,* where she hands over the narrative reins to Marie Antoinette, letting her tell her own story in first person, present tense—letting the unfairly maligned queen become the author of her own narrative, the artist of her own life, including her tragic ending.

The Presence of the Past: Historical Fiction and Fictional History

Let me turn now to the other source of energy and inspiration in Naslund's fiction—the historical imagination. Starting with *Sherlock in Love,* Naslund becomes primarily an historical novelist. *Ahab's Wife, Four Spirits, Abundance*—a particularly ambitious three-book run in contemporary American literature—along with significant portions of *The Fountain of St. James Court* and *Adam and Eve,* all are defined by their focus on often radically different time periods.

History offers a mask for Naslund, a way of telling a deeper truth. She has said, on many occasions, that her historical novels are actually her most spiritually autobiographical works—that Una Spenser, Stella Silver (one of the protagonists of *Four Spirits*), and Marie Antoinette are alter-egos, characters who grant her entry into the past and serve as refracted mirrors of our own times, and of the plight, especially of women, throughout not just literary history but history itself. Of course, the research must be part of the pleasure for Naslund, as it is for most historical novelists—a desire to not just understand the past, as an historian, but to fully *inhabit* it, to clothe oneself in it, to see, smell, taste, touch, and hear it, to dream in it, and to discover the eerie echoes and rhymes in the present moment.

What seems most remarkable to me is how different these books are from one another. If there is a radical difference, in scope and degree of difficulty, between *Ahab's Wife* and the books that came before it, then there is an equally radical difference in structure, style, and strategy in the novels that follow. Over a four-book sequence, she inhabits Victorian London, nineteenth-century New England, Civil Rights-era Alabama, and then the court of Louis XVI and Marie Antoinette in eighteenth-century France. It's enough to give a reader whiplash.

What is even more surprising is not just the shifts in time and place, but the shift in voices, in narrative strategies, in sensibilities. To be sure, there are similarities in theme and authorial obsession: a pervasive inquiry into and advocacy for justice; an argument for kindness, even in the face of hostile, lethal cruelty; deep meditations on and compelling portraits of marriage and friendship; a belief in the waywardness of the human heart; and a profound faith in art, in writing, in education as forces of salvation more powerful than traditional religious belief, though many of her characters are deeply spiritual.

What seems most remarkable to me, however, is the radical shift in the voices authoring these tales. Marie Antoinette's voice is similar to Una's—there's the slightly antique language of a different time—but Una and Marie are entirely different beings, with their own ways of speaking and experiencing the world.

Four Spirits is particularly fascinating to me, and I wish to focus more specifically on it because I believe we can see the seeds of Naslund's historical imagination most clearly here, even though it was her sixth published novel and her third historical novel.

Four Spirits is the most obviously autobiographical of her books. She was born and raised in Birmingham, Alabama, lived as a young woman through that terrible period in the early sixties when Birmingham was the epicenter of racial hostility, with Sheriff Bull Connor unleashing the dogs and turning the hoses on nonviolent protestors to the dismay of the nation, with Martin Luther King, Jr. famously writing his "Letter from Birmingham Jail" to local clergy who had called upon him to not be as aggressive in his direct action campaign and to wait for the "natural" process of change to occur. And then, most shockingly, in 1963, four young black girls were murdered in a church bombing—an event that seems, sadly, all too familiar to us twenty years into the twenty-first century.

These events forged in Naslund a desire to someday tell the story of her home city, to not whitewash or sanitize the history of that time, to celebrate the courage of both the leaders and followers of the nonviolent movement, and to find a way to juxtapose extreme external drama with the deeply felt interior experience of ordinary life, where people get on with the difficult but life-affirming business of courting, of working, of parenting, of going to school, of being in community.

Naslund has said that though she had promised herself, as a young writer, that she would write the story of that period, many decades went by before she did so because she did not believe she had either the artistic maturity or the technical mastery to do the subject justice. She told me that she had once attempted, early in the book's evolution, to wrestle this material into a play, but it didn't work. She wrote many other books, and then while she was on book tour in Australia for *Ahab's Wife*, she learned that one of the men responsible for the bombing of the church was finally being tried for murder. Suddenly, she said, she felt as if that pivotal history from her youth reached through time and galvanized her again, giving her the confidence, urgency, and will to take on the task. If *Ahab's Wife* has the feeling of giddy exuberance on every page, of a writer discovering the grand reach of her talent and the boldness of her narrative premise, *Four Spirits* contains the gravity, resonance, and force of a decades-long promise finally kept.

And if *Ahab's Wife* is Melvillian in both structure and style, *Four Spirits* is indebted structurally and stylistically to, and is in complex conversation with, William Faulkner and Virginia Woolf. The novel has a distinctly modernist sensibility—with its nimble access to the inner lives of a large cast of characters, both fictional and historical, its forgoing of the intentionally heightened language of a narrator-memoirist in favor of a sly rotating omniscience, with catlike leaps into the consciousness of characters who are unaware that the semi-invisible narrative voice is inhabiting and revealing their minds and hearts to the reader, creating a mosaic, a tapestry, in which the whole is much greater than the sum of its parts.

Faulkner's influence is palpable from the beginning, in the first epigraph: "The past isn't dead; it's not even past." Faulkner is also there in the dizzying multitude of characters, calling to mind *As I Lay Dying*, a book to which Naslund acknowledges her indebtedness in the after-notes. Faulkner's influence, however, is most evident in terms of the subject and significance of the novel: the ongoing racial tension in the South; the history of bigotry, segregation, and hatred that has infected the country; and the violence and fear that limns every interaction, especially in the upheavals in Birmingham, with the white establishment's complicity in systemized cruelty and the KKK's terrorist strategies raising the threat-level of even the most quotidian activities—going on a date, attending night school, eating in a restaurant, worshipping at church.

What fascinates me most about this book, other than its gripping moral authority, is Naslund's approach to the technical challenges of her vision, finding ways of adapting her talent to not only a new set of circumstances and cast of characters, but also to learning how to use and then employing an entirely new set of tools for this task. Coming off of *Ahab's Wife*, you would think it would be hard to transition back into the quasi-contemporary world, the world of the mid-twentieth-century South. I would imagine it would be difficult to break free from the nineteenth-century voice that had consumed her consciousness for six years.

Yet here, she chooses a decidedly different point of view, a different style—the free indirect approach of the modernists, especially Virginia Woolf. And assessing her subject as one of community rather than the epic existential quest of an individual, she enlarges her scope and her sympathies, entering into the consciousness of as many characters as she possibly can, even a Klan member and his abused wife, risking narrative fragmentation in service of the larger thematic, emotional, and moral focus of the narrative. This is a book about a community in extreme, destabilizing distress, and therefore the communal voice, the fragmented voice, is the most effective.

Her boldness, in terms of structure and style, in terms of narrative design and voice, derives from her willingness to give up what she's just spent six years perfecting. That relinquishing of what she's just mastered, of not resting on her laurels or remaining in her aesthetic wheelhouse, must have taken enormous artistic courage. It is the same courage we see in each book that follows, radical departures from one another, so much so that what seems most surprising is that the same writer wrote these books. Naslund's artistic distinctiveness derives, in large part, from her ability and willingness to reinvent herself in this way with each project, to bend her talent and her technical skill to the demands of new subjects and new historical moments. And when she doesn't think she possesses the skills or artistic temperament for the task, she works to develop them so that she is able to serve her characters, her unifying themes, and her overarching narrative vision and design.

The great pleasure of doing a deep dive into Naslund's work is watching an artist expanding her repertoire and her range, increasing the degree of difficulty, and then working tirelessly to master those difficulties so the novels seem, to the reader, effortless.

Literary Mothers

One of the most inspiring aspects of working in Spalding's MFA in Writing Program is that for so many years it was directed by a master writer and teacher, one who did not get burned out or become diminished as a writer or teacher, no matter how many years she worked. Instead, she got better, more experimental, more daring, more ambitious and assured in her mission as an artist, yet still humble and courageous enough to keep learning, to reinvent her role within her imagined narratives, to reinvestigate her assumptions, to attempt what she had not tried before. It is particularly inspiring to me, as a longtime creative writing and literature professor myself, to see how she has built this significant body of work while also teaching full-time, sometimes more than full-time—and co-creating a program dedicated to giving writers of any age the opportunity to find their voices, to nurture their literary visions.

Preparing the original lecture, having a reason to delve into Naslund's work and to contemplate her literary and nonliterary influences as well as her influence over me, served as a form of solace and clarity after a few troubling years, when I experienced a life-threatening medical scare and lost two close relatives, including my mother. My mother was about the same age as Naslund. They grew up during the same era, both of them products of the South. Both brilliant women, though the similarity ends there. My mother has been the dark, frequently tragic muse of much of my own writing. I have not consciously sought out Naslund as a surrogate mother, but she has nevertheless served as a different kind of model and muse for me. What I discovered and admired afresh in her body of work, as I plunged more deeply into it, is what I have found in Naslund the person, the colleague, the boss, the traveling companion—a woman and a writer of extraordinary kindness and resiliency and an advocate for gentleness and forgiveness.

She has reminded me of the power of fiction, of literature, of art, of education to heal the spirit. Literature has saved my life many times over the years, as I imagined it has saved the lives of many of you reading this essay. Still, we all need reminders that literature still has that spiritual power, that uncanny ability to heal and inspire. With her work and by the honorable example of her life, Naslund reminds me of that, and I am grateful. My fellow Spalding colleagues, students, and alumni are fortunate to have been the beneficiaries of the program that Naslund envisioned, that *Ahab's Wife* built, a program rooted in literary friendship and a commitment to fostering not only artistic excellence, intellectual rigor, frankness ("Now let's talk turkey!"), and technical virtuosity, but more importantly the emotional courage and ecstasy that we all need to do our best work, to be our best selves, to be the authors of our own lives, and to do so in order to make the world seem a less lonely and more intentionally just and joyful place.

My Hamlet

I was seventeen the first time I encountered Hamlet in performance. I remember late one night, all of us from the two Amarillo High School honors classes watching the BBC version of *Hamlet*, with Derek Jacobi as Hamlet, Claire Bloom as Gertrude, and a bushy-headed Patrick Stewart (pre-Jean-Luc Picard) as Claudius. It was a warm November evening when we entered the building. When we emerged five hours later, it was snowing. Mr. Huber, our charismatic English teacher, looked up and said, "It's only fitting that the seasons should change because of *Hamlet*."

Dwight Huber loved Shakespeare, and he taught us to love him as well through his insistent questioning, his demand that we substantiate everything by specific reference to the text. He expected us to demonstrate mastery over what we had read. He forced us to think aloud, on our feet, and to assert what we felt and thought and then to examine those emotions and ideas carefully so that mysterious, transcendent epiphanies seemed to hover in the air of the classroom, within our grasp.

One of the great and sobering lessons I learned from Mr. Huber that year concerned *Hamlet*. Although he could be ruthless with his red pen, he was almost always good humored with us in class, enthusiastically and lavishly praising our insights—"Yes, you are *absolutely* right, Melanie!"; "*Brilliant*, Trish!"—and careful never to humiliate us, or dismiss our half-baked ideas, or show signs of exasperation, anger, or condescension. Yet early on in our discussions of *Hamlet,* maybe the first or second day, he grew unexpectedly upset with us. We had not read the play carefully or were perhaps too whimsical, cracking jokes, not very eager to get down to the important business of explication, analysis, and the aesthetics of suffering. He spoke very little during our shenanigans.

About midway through the class period, he said in a calm voice that I'll never forget, a voice that did not mask his contempt: "*Hamlet* deserves better than this." Then he sat down at his desk and began grading papers, ignoring us until the bell rang. We were all dumbfounded. A couple of us tried to make a joke, but he did not acknowledge it, and we soon opened our books and hid ourselves in our silent explorations of the play.

We were stunned and ashamed, I believe, not only because we had never seen this side of him, but also because we knew that we had let him down. We respected—indeed loved—him too much to want to do that. We understood that we had taken his good nature for granted, that this was personal for him. But what also surprised me then—and still resonates with me now more than three dozen years later—were his actual words. He didn't say, "*I* deserve better than this" or "*You* can do better than this." What he said was: "*Hamlet* deserves better than this."

It was unclear whether he meant the play or the character, *Hamlet* or Hamlet, but either way, his anger was not about ego—his or ours. Nor did he say it in a pedantic way. He was the antithesis of a pedant and could be just as ridiculous—dancing a jig, making a joke, contorting his face into a clown's mask, singing a ditty—as we were. Nevertheless, Hamlet and *Hamlet* deserved our very best, he suggested with his comment and his icy contempt, and anything less was disrespectful not only to ourselves and to him as our teacher, but to the experience that Shakespeare had bestowed upon us all. Mr. Huber was, in effect, defending Shakespeare's honor, defending Hamlet's honor, defending *Hamlet's* honor.

When we resumed our discussion the next day, we soared. It was clear we'd all gone home and immersed ourselves in the play, had made ourselves vulnerable to what both Hamlet and *Hamlet* had to teach us—the Prince's deep ambivalence about the mandate issued by the ghost of his father, his violent disillusionment with Ophelia and his mother and the political and emotional rottenness in Denmark, his meditations on suicide and the futility of action, his histrionic despair as he leaps into Ophelia's grave, and then the cathartic calm that descends on the play with his death, as flights of angels sing this sweet prince to his rest. We brought that experience and enthusiasm back to Mr. Huber and to each other, as if proffering a delicate gift.

Looking back, I can see why *Hamlet* affected me so deeply then. I had the uncanny feeling that Shakespeare was talking directly to me. I had struggled with the text, which seemed dense and at times impenetrable, in class and at home. But watching the play, even this flawed BBC production, the characters and story miraculously emerged, as if from a fog-shrouded forest of language, and I suddenly saw and felt my own life refracted in it.

My parents had divorced for the second and final time when I was in fifth grade, and my mother, sister, and I had moved from Houston to Amarillo. My mother had remarried not once, but four times while I was in middle school and high school, and the stepfathers and other men who had come into our home were often violent and at times, it seemed to me and my sister, murderous.

Like Hamlet, I secretly wondered if I was a coward, unable to adequately protect my mother and sister from the threat and trauma, desiring to escape from the chaos, especially on those occasions when my mother desperately begged me to kill two of her husbands. Like Hamlet, I felt miscast in, and ill-equipped for, a revenge tragedy. I wanted to be a courtier, a running back, a sprinter, a lawyer, a scholar. Not an avenging angel, not the scourge of justice. *O curséd spite,/ That ever I was born to set it right.* I knew that feeling intimately.

After my mother, sister, and I moved with her fifth husband to Amarillo, my father felt free to relocate to Las Vegas, where he became a ghost in the great American limbo city. We rarely heard from, much less saw, him for several years. But during my junior year in high school, I called him one winter night, desperate after yet another encounter with one of my mother's drunken lovers, and asked for his help, in fact begged him for escape. He reluctantly invited me to live with him for the summer, a summer that shifted the course of my life, a summer I spent floating in his apartment complex pool, writing bad poetry which I shared with his girlfriend, a dental hygienist, and reading the collected essays of Ralph Waldo Emerson.

As I prepared to fly home to Texas at the end of the summer, my father and I talked about my returning to Las Vegas for college, and after that going to law school, and then eventually joining him in his new business, perhaps as, he jokingly said, his *consiglieri*. What that business was, I didn't really know. My father and mother had owned cosmetics and lingerie businesses. He was a successful carpet salesman for several years, and then he had somehow morphed into a con-man who had once, according to family lore, tried to buy Costa Rica. He was terrified of the government and justice system. His brother was in prison for international mail fraud. My father had come to Las Vegas to seek his fortune, which he believed was just around the corner, and during the summer I spent with him, we spent a lot of time contemplating our glorious future together.

During that first introduction to *Hamlet*, I saw all too clearly my life embodied in the young prince's dilemma—an adolescent romantically idealizing his absent father, disillusioned by his mother's "o'er hasty" marriages, and secretly afraid of being forced to do something courageous to radically change the situation.

I was fortunate to have great Shakespeare teachers. Not only Dwight Huber but my undergraduate Shakespeare professor, Dr. Charmazel Dudt, a tall, imposing woman from India with a musical accent and booming laugh, a woman who wore a bright sari every class and expertly guided my peers and me through the Shakespearean canon in two courses (Early Plays, Late Plays) and presided over my first serious critical efforts, including an essay on the disease imagery in *Hamlet,* others on the multiplot dynamics of the *Henry IV & V* plays, the fool in *Twelfth Night,* and my magnum opus of undergraduate literary criticism on Shakespeare's conception of time in *Macbeth* and *Hamlet*, an essay that launched me into graduate school.

I was also a theatre major, working on more than thirty productions as an undergraduate, taking acting classes with a theatre professor who eventually became my father-in-law, performing scenes from *Hamlet*, among other plays. I dreamed at that time of becoming a Shakespearean actor or perhaps a Shakespearean scholar.

But when I was twenty-two, in my first year of graduate school, studying literature, my father died of a massive heart attack on the steps of a Las Vegas hospital room, and that event altered my life. *Hamlet*—that play obsessed with dead fathers and grief-stricken sons—vibrated with new and painful meanings. My father's death eventually drove me away from the scholar's life. I spent my first year of doctoral studies neglecting my literature classes, taking permanent incompletes in my Chaucer and nineteenth-century British Literature seminars, immersing myself instead in the world of the theatre, where my wife was pursuing her doctorate, directing and acting in plays, performing in an improvisational comedy troupe, and having much more fun than I was.

I did nine shows that year, including a turn as Mercutio in a post-holocaust *Romeo and Juliet* (my highwater mark as a Shakespearean actor) and a glorious summer of repertory theatre, and then left my doctoral program for my first faculty position, teaching four sections each semester of composition and literature as a visiting instructor at the

College of Charleston. The death of my father intensified my hunger to tell my own stories and the stories of my family, whose tales would be lost forever, I believed, if somebody didn't record and try to make sense of them. I yearned to do that rather than spend my life as a scholar, chasing footnotes.

While teaching at the College of Charleston, I started and finished my MFA, an experience that launched me into my life as a creative writer as well as my dream job at a small iconoclastic college in Prescott, Arizona, where I got to teach pretty much whatever I wanted—a full slate of fiction writing and other creative writing courses, as well any literature or interdisciplinary course that I thought would help me and my students become better readers and writers—among them, Literature of the American Dream, the American West in Film and Literature, Travel Writing, Family Systems in Film and Literature, Literature as Experience, Dramatic Literature, and Shakespeare.

The twenty-one years I taught at Prescott College were rich and thrilling years of my teaching life. Shakespeare was, in many ways, at the center of it, and *Hamlet* was at the heart of the Shakespeare seminar, the culminating text that we would spend a month studying. I took my students on field trips to see Shakespeare productions in Phoenix, Flagstaff, Tucson, and Sedona. I showed them many film adaptations of the plays, analyzing up to eight different versions of individual scenes. My students wrote critical analyses and research papers but also their own Shakespeare-inspired scenes, soliloquies, plays, stories, poems, personal essays, and songs. Every other year, when I taught the seminar, I re-immersed myself in the plays and sonnets, in the long and complicated history of criticism, and in the rich theatrical and cinematic history.

As I wrote my first published books—a novel and stories inspired largely by my ne'er-do-well working-class Texas family, but more influenced by Shakespeare than anyone would guess—my wife, kids, and I began to make yearly pilgrimages, seven hours away, to the Utah Shakespeare Festival, one of the great classical repertory companies in the country, a company that later won a Tony as the best regional theatre. I even traveled with the artistic directors and other patrons on a theatre tour of Ireland and London and spent a more extended period at the Utah festival with my wife when she was a playwright-in-residence and one of her plays was given an extended workshop and staged reading.

At some point during this time, I fell out of love with *Hamlet*—partly because of my dissatisfaction with the cinematic and theatrical performances of the play, none of which matched the combined grandeur and intimacy of the text in my imagination. But I also became unaccountably irritated with and then bored by Shakespeare's melodrama and felt resentful of and saddened by my irritation and boredom. In fact, I developed an outright antipathy toward the tragedy. My whole course was designed with *Hamlet* as the culminating event, yet I dreaded teaching it. I kept thinking of this deliciously nasty poem by D. H. Lawrence, the working-class skeptic, wary of the eloquent bombast of princes and kings:

WHEN I READ SHAKESPEARE

When I read Shakespeare I am struck with wonder
that such trivial people should muse and thunder
in such lovely language.

Lear, the old buffer, you wonder his daughters
didn't treat him rougher,
the old chough, the old chuffer!

And Hamlet, how boring, boring to live with,
so mean and self-conscious, blowing and snoring
his wonderful speeches, full of other folks' whoring!

And Macbeth and his Lady, who should have been choring,
such suburban ambition, so messily goring
old Duncan with Daggers!

How boring and small Shakespeare's people are!
Yet the language so lovely! like the dyes from gas-tar.

Hamlet and Hamlet (both the play and the character) seemed suddenly quite stupid to me, even embarrassing. D. H. Lawrence was right. Hamlet, how boring, so mean and self-conscious, a blowhard, gaseous, a case of arrested development, overly concerned with "other folks' whoring."

Why was this Shakespeare's iconic play? You can see some of my residual antipathy represented in my churlish description for the lecture (which eventually became this essay) that I was asked to give during a residency for Spalding University's low-residency MFA in Writing Program in 2016, part of the city of Louisville's celebration of the four-hundredth anniversary of Shakespeare's death, called "Will in the 'Ville":

> Why *Hamlet*? It's not Shakespeare's most lyrical or perfectly constructed play. It's not as riveting as *Othello* or *Macbeth*. It doesn't have the grandeur of *King Lear* or the tear-jerking romance of *Romeo and Juliet*. The plot and characters—with sibling murder, an angry, jealous ghost mandating vengeance, an offstage encounter with pirates, eight deaths, and a baffling, brooding, inconsistent protagonist morbidly obsessed with his mother's sex life—are melodramatic and sometimes ludicrous. Unlike most of Shakespeare's plays, which he seemed to write quickly, there's evidence that Shakespeare may have written and revised this play extensively

over a decade, never quite satisfied. There are odd digressions and abrupt tonal shifts. The full-length version is overwritten and almost always radically cut for performance. The secondary characters don't have the vitality or complexity of those in Shakespeare's other great plays. So what makes *Hamlet* great? Why does this idiosyncratic, misshapen, weirdly personal drama continue to speak to us?

In truth, I increasingly found the play to be bloated, full of histrionics and unnecessary cruelty and a Freudian reductivism that sickened me. I felt that Shakespeare (and self-proclaimed Bardolators such as Harold Bloom) pled too much for Hamlet, who seemed increasingly like the narcissistic delinquent that Tom Stoppard depicts in his famous riff on the play, *Rosencrantz and Guildenstern Are Dead*.

This period of antipathy toward both the play and Hamlet as a character, I should mention, may have had something to do with the fact that my four children, especially my oldest son, were entering their teenage years, and I found myself saturated with adolescent angst, melancholy, mood swings, and paranoia. I empathized with the parents in the play—Claudius, Gertrude, and Polonius, even the Elder Hamlet, who returns to "chide" his procrastinating son.

I still loved teaching Shakespeare. But other plays seized my imagination more forcefully, especially *Othello* and the history plays involving Falstaff and Prince Hal, *Twelfth*

Night and *Romeo and Juliet*, *The Merchant of Venice* and *King Lear*, more naturalistic plays which benefited from excellent contemporary film and theatrical productions. I still went out of my way to see new productions of *Hamlet:* the David Tennant/Patrick Stewart BBC production; Jude Law on Broadway; a good production at the Stratford, Ontario festival; another strong one at the Utah Shakespeare Festival, starring its future artistic director, Brian Vaughn; and a National Theatre production with Benedict Cumberbatch. But the play no longer gripped my imagination in the same, intensely personal way. I couldn't get past the artificiality of the performances, which made me cringe. Even when a performance was successful, it was invariably the secondary characters—Ophelia and Gertrude, Claudius and Polonius, Laertes, the Gravedigger, even the nearly invisible Fortinbras, prowling around the fringes—who seemed more compelling to me.

But in 2015, *Hamlet* reentered my imagination with a sudden and eerily disturbing force. Several events triggered this shift in my perspective. That year my uncle, who was like a brother to me, my best friend and best man at my wedding—my uncle-brother, I sometimes called him, in a comic inversion of Hamlet's reference to Claudius as his "uncle-father"—died of complications related to lung cancer, which had debilitated him over several years, especially after several intensive-care emergencies.

During this period of grief, I found myself also crippled by self-doubt about my creative abilities. A long, 150,000-word novel inspired by my father's life, which I started in my early forties at the age he was when he died of his heart attack, had stalled. In fact, it more than stalled. I considered it a catastrophic failure—a decade-long, multi-draft disaster. To fix it, I knew I would need to completely reconceive the book, perhaps start over. But was it worth it? Did I have the time or energy or clarity or will to do it?

The answer, though I was terrified to admit it to myself or anyone else, seemed painfully obvious at the time: *No.*

I had been trying to resign myself to that failure, as I turned my attention to other book projects, including collections of poetry, stories, and essays, and an ambitious trilogy of novels set in an Arizona Shakespeare festival, another passion project I'd been nursing along for several years. But still, I felt as if I had not only failed as an artist, but as if I had failed my father, or rather the promise I had made to myself when I began my writing career—that I would someday write him into the world again, tell his story so he wouldn't be consigned to oblivion.

I decided to bury the book and get on with my life and turn my attention to these other more promising, less emotionally exhausting projects.

But it wasn't that simple. As I tried to bury the book, my father began to haunt my dreams. I couldn't shake free of his face (so similar to mine), or his voice, or the way he cackled when he laughed, the way he twisted his hair into knots as he haggled on the phone with "chumps" he was trying to sell something to, the way he looked in his coffin, dressed ridiculously in a black kimono, chopsticks and his favorite coffee mug placed by his second wife, a Japanese woman, on the pillow next to his head.

My father was suddenly always there in my consciousness, and at night I feared sleep. On more than one occasion, I woke at two, three, four in the morning with pinpricks of pain in my chest and left arm. Phantom pains? Warning signs? I didn't know which. I began eating Tums by the roll to fight what I tried to convince myself was simply indigestion. I'd had a scare a decade earlier, which landed me in the ER, only to discover that my phantom heart attack had been merely pepperoni-pizza-induced heartburn.

Still, during this time, I couldn't stop thinking about *Hamlet*, especially Shakespeare's obsession with the ghosts of dead fathers. I reread the play, the first time in several years. The play no longer seemed ridiculous or embarrassing to me. It was, instead, terrifying.

Although I'd seen, studied, and/or taught the play probably a hundred times, I found myself swallowed by it anew and wanted a fresh audience of students, colleagues, fellow writers, tavern drunks, anyone who would let me tell them what I now understood about this play, as if I was the first one to discover its bottomless brilliance, its mysteriously uncanny wisdom.

I wanted to explain how the play is a deep meditation on madness and suicide, on revenge and honor, on the outlandish mandates that fathers give sons. It's about brothers killing brothers, beginning before the play opens with Claudius committing not just regicide but fratricide against the Elder Hamlet and ending with young Hamlet killing his schoolboy brothers, Rosencrantz and Guildenstern, and then Hamlet and Laertes killing each other, arrows shot over the symbolic brothers' houses. I wanted to talk about ghost stories and the deconstruction of revenge tragedies. I wanted to talk about the way this play, like all of Shakespeare's plays, is a secrecy plot, and how secrets always yearn for revelations, and revelations feed reckonings, and reckonings demand moral, emotional, psychological, and spiritual recalibrations.

I wanted to demonstrate how the play is a treatise on espionage, on eavesdropping and spying, how it's about mildewed ears and busybodies who get themselves stabbed, about sting operations and the way "indirection finds directions out," and how "deep plots do pall," and how these failures teach us that "there's providence in the fall of a sparrow," and "a divinity that shapes our ends, rough-hew them how we will."

I wanted to talk about the terrible rap women get in this play—jigging and ambling and lisping, honeying and stewing over the nasty sty, too green or frail or carnal to figure out what is happening to those around them, doomed puppets for the men who control them—driven into real madness, drinking the lake water or the poisoned wine, forced to look inside their grainy hearts.

I wanted to talk about conceptual and experimental innovators—how Shakespeare is primarily a conceptual innovator, working brilliantly and fast, producing thirty-six plays in less than twenty years, not to mention the hundred and fifty or so sonnets and the long poems, all the while co-owning, acting for, and helping to operate a thriving theatre. And yet *Hamlet,* as a play, appears to be the exception for Shakespeare, a case of experimental innovation, a play he may have rewritten over a ten-year period and one that seems strangely specific and personal, especially given the deaths, near the time of the first performance, of his father as well as his only son, the eerily named Hamnet.

I wanted to talk about the soliloquies, about Hamlet's embassy of death, about radical excision, and how Shakespeare, through *Hamlet,* invents the human, as Harold Bloom too grandly claims, by capturing characters in the act of overhearing themselves think. I wanted, in particular, to talk about the "to be or not to be" soliloquy, and the radical difference between the Quartos and the First Folio, and why this contemplation of suicide has entered, rightly or wrongly, into popular culture as the most famous speech in literature.

And I wanted to dissect the nunnery scene—the stunning opening of Act Three in which Ophelia returns Hamlet's gifts, and he viciously turns on her once he realizes she is the bait to lure him into a confession about his motives. The scene, I wanted to say to anyone who would listen to me, radically upends our idea of who Hamlet is, pivots him away from the meditative paralysis of "to be or not to be" toward paranoia and cruelty, and metastasizes his vision of Denmark transformed from a sacred into a profane world—a transformation epitomized by the double meaning of the word "nunnery" as both convent and brothel, the place he consigns Ophelia. And I wanted to talk about the heartbreaking collapse of Ophelia, whose own mind is "jangled out of tune" by these events, turning her from sweetness and naiveté to derangement, from flowers and prettiness, as her brother says, to death, sex, and the defiled body. A genuine portrait of insanity which counterpoints and gives visceral expression to Hamlet's fears about his own insipient madness.

Hamlet's line near the end of the play kept floating into my head, like the refrain of a song I could not stop listening to: "how ill all's here about my heart—but it is no matter."

I talked to my physician, who instructed me to get a stress test. I put the test off, unwilling to face the bad news or half-believing that, by avoiding the test, I wouldn't have to deal with the reckoning. The Christmas holidays came, and the pinpricks and indigestion temporarily disappeared. Or I simply refused to acknowledge their seriousness.

As 2016 began, there were other stressors in my life, none more alarming than my younger sister's plight. She had suffered the most in our family, left behind while I went to college, as the violence and turmoil in my mother's home worsened and as my father, resettled in Las Vegas, distanced himself from us all. My sister had dropped out of high school in tenth grade, was a mother by age sixteen (the same year my father died), a drug addict by eighteen. She'd recovered in her twenties and thirties, married a couple more times, had another child and three grandchildren, but now, at age forty-seven, found herself alone, uneducated, without health insurance, and with the prospect of an increasingly bleak future.

She got in a car wreck, was laid off from her fourteen-year job as an office manager, was charged with a DUI, left her belongings in a storage locker in Tyler, Texas, and moved back to Amarillo in January, where she immediately fell into an alcoholic freefall that seemed to all of us looking helplessly on like a slow-motion suicide. By early February, she'd practically stopped eating, dropped to ninety pounds, but continued (we learned later) to drown herself in vodka. She began hallucinating, wielding butcher knives, became so dangerous that she could not be trusted around children, including her own grandchildren, and had to be placed nightly by her son and her childhood best friend in various homeless and women's shelters, where she went AWOL one night and had her car and most of her money, including her small severance package, stolen.

I had a terrifying phone conversation with her during this time. She was hallucinating, jabbering, high as a kite or completely crazy or both, and the words throughout the conversation that I could not get out of my mind were Laertes' bewildered, heart-rending ones in the fourth act, upon seeing his radically transformed sister: A "document in madness." For several days, my family lost my sister, literally lost her, until we discovered that she had committed herself to a psychiatric hospital, where she stayed, thankfully, for a week, detoxing.

I found myself during this time obsessed with the circumstances surrounding my father's heart attack and his strange and harrowing funeral. I wrote and relentlessly revised—during a short writing retreat in northern California—an essay about that traumatic experience, along with chapters from the failed novel about my father that I converted into free-standing short stories.

Exhausted, creatively and emotionally spent, but exhilarated too by the exorcism, I sent these pieces out to literary journals before leaving California—the first manuscripts I'd sent unsolicited to journals in several years.

A week and half later, near the end of March, the heart attack that I had been fearing for the last decade, and had been secretly dreading for the last six months, finally arrived—nearly thirty years to the day of the heart attack that killed my father.

I thought at first it was indigestion again. I'd just eaten a take-home dinner from my favorite Mexican food restaurant and inexplicably chased it down with two glasses of orange juice: a recipe for acid reflux. My wife was in Arizona, visiting our friends in Prescott before heading to an academic conference in Los Angeles. Two of my kids, neither of whom could drive, were at home with me. My oldest daughter was at a theatre rehearsal.

The pressure in my chest would not go away after five, ten, fifteen minutes.

I didn't want to scare my children, but as a precaution, I drove myself to the hospital. Halfway there, I realized my mistake. Moaning in the car, my kids on the speaker phone listening to me, I stumbled, after a series of near-catastrophic driving and parking errors, into the ER, where they quickly conducted tests and confirmed I was indeed having a major heart attack that required immediate surgery. When I asked the nurses and doctors ringed about me if I was going to die, they all looked down or away, deliberately ignoring my question. That's when I realized the severity of my situation.

They loaded me in an ambulance and raced me to Mercy Hospital in Des Moines, thirty-five miles away. I made my final deathbed calls to my children and wife along the way, everything boiled down to a simple, throat-clotted "I love you." At the hospital, a team of cackling nurses stripped me and quickly shaved my groin, and the cardiac surgeon, a man who looked like Mr. Rogers, assured me, when I asked him if I was going to die, that he would do his best to make sure that didn't happen.

The day after my heart attack, as I recovered in the hospital's cardiac intensive care unit, my sister was transferred from the psychiatric hospital in Amarillo into a faith-based rehab program for indigent women and began a month-long blackout period in which she was not allowed to have contact with the world.

A week later, I was back at work, shaken and confused, not able to wrap my head around what had just occurred to both me and my sister, our miraculous escape from the separate but simultaneous tragedies that should have claimed our lives.

In the months after, during my cardiac rehab, I found myself obsessed with *Hamlet,* and began studying it again. I felt, as I had felt more than three decades before, when I first read and watched the play, that it was speaking directly to me. "To be or not to be" no longer seemed like a pretty speech about existential decision-making, but rather a question that was and is still intimately and excruciatingly mine and my family's. Convalescing, I kept reading and rereading the fifth act of the play, especially the scene in the churchyard, where the comedy of the Gravedigger gives way to, at first, an abstract meditation on death (dead tanners and lawyers), and then to something increasingly more intimate ("Alas, poor Yorick"), until Hamlet leaps crazily with Laertes into the yawning grave where Ophelia's body lies.

Those speeches by the Elder Hamlet's ghost no longer were artificial, lugubrious, or ridiculous. As a father of four, I found myself needing to hear from the ghost of a father (a role Shakespeare himself played) who left the world too early—"cut off even in the blossoms of [his] sin." I wanted to know more than ever what advice that ghost had to give to his child and try to ferret out what his own motives were. I now knew what it felt like to be on the other side, to be that ghost, to exist in a state of limbo, vulnerable and confused, between this world and the next, too eager to rectify the world I've left or will leave behind, too anxious to warn my wife and children how they should live without me.

There is a happy ending to this story.

Though she still struggles with her addictions, my sister is doing better. I got to spend time with her later that October and November—our first time together since our simultaneous rock-bottom flirtations with death. A year after her entry into the program, she "graduated" from the "nunnery," as I took to calling it, and she is in the process of reconstructing her life, dreaming now, after all these deferred decades, of going to college to become a drug and alcohol counselor, to help those who have been where she has been, to keep others from drowning, as she nearly did.

And I am, in many ways, healthier than I've been in a long while. I eat better. I exercise every day. I'm skinnier. I've grown my hair long, as I like to tell my wife and friends and children and students, for my future Shakespearean roles. I take medication to thin my blood and keep my cholesterol and blood pressure in check.

I can now joke about the heart attack with my wife, kids, and closest friends. I've been to Europe and back, including a month in London and Stratford-upon-Avon, where I co-taught with my wife a study abroad course only three months after my heart attack, and where we saw fifteen plays, including two shows at the Royal Shakespeare Company and three thrilling productions, as a groundling—of *Macbeth, A Midsummer Night's Dream,* and an Irish-inflected *Taming of the Shrew*—all of us, me especially, enthralled and smiling with delight near the lip of the Globe Theatre stage.

On my keyring, I carry nitroglycerin for emergencies and have only had to slip the pills under my tongue on a few occasions, including one scary evening in Paris in the shadow of the Eiffel Tower, when I was mistakenly convinced again I was on the verge of another heart attack.

And most importantly, I am writing again—with urgency and, for the first time in a long time, with genuine joy. I feel I can no longer indulge myself with decades-long writing projects. I am eager to finish my work while I still have time.

These are the lines from *Hamlet* that resonate with me most fully now, the words the mystical fifth-act Hamlet tells Horatio, as he contemplates the inevitable fate that he knows awaits him:

> If it be not now, 'tis not to come. If it be not to come, it will be now. If it be not now, yet it will come. The readiness is all. Since no man, of aught he leaves, knows aught, what is't to leave betimes? Let be.

I have understood for a long time—as a passionate student and longtime teacher of Shakespeare—that *Hamlet* is literature's most famous and profound poem about death. It is the journey from "to be or not to be" to "let be." The odyssey from anxiety and paralysis to emotional and spiritual readiness.

But I didn't feel in my body or in my spirit the significance of that journey until 2016. I sense that *Hamlet*—that shadow text that has hovered so close to me for my entire adult life, as an ally and talisman and for the last few years as a haunted intruder—reentered my imagination in order to teach me how to die. I am grateful for the teaching, even if I am not quite ready to go.

The rest—for me, for all of us—is indeed only silence. But I hope not yet.

When I was in Stratford-upon-Avon in 2016, not long after my heart attack, I made a special pilgrimage to Holy Trinity Church, where Shakespeare is buried. I talked another pilgrim into snapping a picture of me in front of Shakespeare's tomb. Shakespeare died four hundred years ago that spring. He was, like me at the time, only fifty-two.

Acknowledgments

Earlier versions of some of these essays were published in the following: "Narrative Strategy and Dramatic Design" in *The Writer's Chronicle;* "On the Road: The Do-It-Yourself Book Tour" in *Poets & Writers* and revised and reprinted for *The Poets & Writers Guide to Publicity and Promotion*; "A Family Theme, a Family Secret" in *Now Write: Fiction Writing Exercises from Today's Best Writers and Teachers* (Ed. Sherry Ellis, Tarcher/Penguin) and reprinted in the *Glimmer Train* Bulletin; "The Pleasures of Form" in the *Glimmer Train* Bulletin; "The Origins of *The Girl from Charnelle*" in the paperback version of *The Girl from Charnelle* (Harper Perennial); "Every Story is a Love Song," "The Habits of Art," and "What We Talk About When We Talk About Influence" in Spalding University's MFA Program in Writing's faculty blog; and "The Secret Story" in *Bloom*.

"My *Hamlet*" was delivered as a plenary lecture for Spalding University as part of the City of Louisville's "Will in the 'Ville," its 2016 celebration of the 400th anniversary of Shakespeare's death. "Sena Jeter Naslund and the Ecstasy of Influence" was the keynote address of Spalding University's 2017 "SenaFest" celebration. "The Art of Disobedience: Twenty Ways to Misbehave" was delivered as a plenary lecture at Spalding University and at the "Desert Nights, Rising Stars" Conference at Arizona State University. I have given many presentations, classes, and workshops on "The Cyclical Imagination" and its underlying research, including panels for conferences held by the Association of Writers and Writing Programs (AWP) and *The North American Review*.

These essays are indebted to many people. I have been blessed with great teachers: Joan Silber, Robert Boswell, Jean Thompson, Dwight Huber, Charmazel Dudt, Sue Park, Russell Sparling, and my father-in-law, Larry Menefee. Richard Russo encouraged my first attempts at fiction years ago, served as the mentor for both my MA thesis and my MFA thesis, convinced me that I could write fiction, and has remained a model of literary and teaching excellence and generosity.

I was fortunate to teach creative writing and literature for two decades at Prescott College in Arizona, and I am grateful to my students and colleagues there for their good company and the opportunity to explore with them many of the ideas in these essays. In particular, I wish to thank Sheila Sanderson, Melanie Bishop, Reuben Ellis, the late Glendon Brunk, Allyson Stack, Julie Hensley, Bob Johnson, and Susan Lang. In 2013, I joined the faculty at Iowa State University. I am grateful to my students and colleagues in Ames, with special thanks to Debra Marquart, Brianna Burke, David Zimmerman, Christiana Langenberg, Ned Balbo, Steve Pett, and Mary Swander.

In 2004, Sena Jeter Naslund welcomed me into the Spalding University MFA faculty, which has been one of the richest literary communities of my life. Many of the essays in this collection were first given as lectures there. Thanks to all my Spalding students and colleagues, especially Kathleen Driskell, Katy Yocom, Karen Mann, Roy Hoffman, Helena Kriel, John Pipkin, Kira Obolensky, Robin Lippincott, Silas House, Crystal Wilkinson, the late Phil Deaver, Richard Goodman, Rachel Harper, Jody Lisberger, Dianne Aprile, Luke Wallin, Julie Brickman, Kirby Gann, Elaine Neil Orr, Leslie Daniels, Greg Pape, Jeannie Thompson, Neela Vaswani, and Terry Price.

Also my appreciation to Steve Semken and Ice Cube Press for your ongoing support of this and other books. To Charles Baxter and Ellen Bryant Voigt, who modeled what lectures and essays on craft could be. And to Nan Cuba, who gave me opportunities at Gemini Ink to teach multi-day workshops on sudden fiction and short story cycles and then later invited me to co-teach a graduate seminar with her on the short story cycle at Our Lady of the Lake University.

The richness of my thirty-year friendship, collaboration, and correspondence with Joseph M. Schuster is inscribed in each of these essays, and I appreciate his comments on the individual pieces and the collection as a whole. Thank you, Wayne Regina and Tim Crews, writing retreat partners for twenty years, and Ronald Regina, for lending us his homes for so many of those retreats.

Special thanks to my children—Vivian, Carson, Lena, and Tristan—for thousands of spirited discussions of fiction, theatre,

Shakespeare, films, television, art, politics, ethics, morality, genre, and aesthetics. How lucky I am to have such fierce debaters and inspiring artists and art-lovers as children. Charissa Menefee has for the past three dozen years broadened, deepened, and challenged my understanding of artmaking and aesthetic form and has been the most significant influence on every aspect of my life and work.

K. L. Cook is the author of four books of fiction: *Last Call*, winner of the Prairie Schooner Book Prize; *The Girl from Charnelle*, winner of the Willa Award for Contemporary Fiction; *Love Songs for the Quarantined*, winner of the Spokane Prize for Short Fiction; and *Marrying Kind*, a new collection of linked stories. *Lost Soliloquies*, a collection of poetry, was also recently published. His work has appeared widely in anthologies, literary journals, and magazines, including *Best American Mystery Stories, Best of the West, Glimmer Train Stories, American Short Fiction, One Story, Harvard Review, Threepenny Review, Writer's Chronicle,* and *Poets & Writers*. He teaches in the MFA Program in Creative Writing & Environment at Iowa State University and the School of Creative and Professional Writing at Spalding University. For more information, visit his author website at www.klook.net.

The Ice Cube Press began publishing in 1991 to focus on how to live with the natural world and to better understand how people can best live together in the communities they share and inhabit. Using the literary arts to explore life and experiences in the heartland of the United States we have been recognized by a number of well-known writers including: Bill Bradley, Gary Snyder, Gene Logsdon, Wes Jackson, Patricia Hampl, Greg Brown, Jim Harrison, Annie Dillard, Ken Burns, Roz Chast, Jane Hamilton, Daniel Menaker, Kathleen Norris, Janisse Ray, Craig Lesley, Alison Deming, Harriet Lerner, Richard Lynn Stegner, Richard Rhodes, Michael Pollan, David Abram, David Orr, and Barry Lopez. We've published a number of well-known authors including: Mary Swander, Jim Heynen, Mary Pipher, Bill Holm, Connie Mutel, John T. Price, Carol Bly, Marvin Bell, Debra Marquart, Ted Kooser, Stephanie Mills, Bill McKibben, Craig Lesley, Elizabeth McCracken, Derrick Jensen, Dean Bakopoulos, Rick Bass, Linda Hogan, Pam Houston, and Paul Gruchow. Check out Ice Cube Press books on our web site, join our email list, Facebook group, or follow us on Twitter. Visit booksellers, museum shops, or any place you can find good books and support true honest to goodness independent publishing projects so you can discover why we continue striving to "hear the other side."

Ice Cube Press, LLC (Est. 1991)
North Liberty, Iowa, Midwest, USA
Resting above the Silurian and Jordan aquifers
steve@icecubepress.com
check us out on twitter and facebook
www.icecubepress.com

To Fenna Marie
an artful force of strength and courage
To Ingrid and your
glorious disobediences.